ARE WE FREE AND INDEPENDENT CREATURES — OR ARE WE PROGRAMMED BY A HOST OF OUTSIDE INFLUENCES TO ACT AND FEEL AS WE DO?

Today this has become one of the vital questions in psychology, as the traditional view of human beings as self-contained units has shown itself to be limited in both the analysis and the alteration of human behavior.

Recently the work of B. F. Skinner, perhaps the world's leading behavioral psychologist, set off a storm of debate when he proposed a society in which the concept of free will had no place, and in which human beings could be molded to fit social design.

On another front, therapists have turned to behavioral methods in treating neuroses, and in parental learning programs, avoiding the often impractical length and uncertain results of other therapeutic approaches.

A PRIMER OF BEHAVIORAL PSYCHOLOGY offers a history and an explanation of this fascinating branch of science, and an opportunity for each reader to ponder its truth and far-reaching implications.

ABOUT THE AUTHOR: ADELAIDE BRY is a trained psychologist, as well as the author of *Inside Psychotherapy, How to Get Angry Without Feeling Guilty,* and *The Sexually Aggressive Woman,* all available in Signet editions.

SIGNET and MENTOR Books of Interest

A PRIMER
OF
BEHAVIORAL
PSYCHOLOGY

Adelaide Bry

A MENTOR BOOK

NEW AMERICAN LIBRARY

TIMES MIRROR
NEW YORK AND SCARBOROUGH, ONTARIO
THE NEW ENGLISH LIBRARY LIMITED, LONDON

For Max Gartenberg, agent and friend

COPYRIGHT © 1975 BY ADELAIDE BRY

Library of Congress Catalog Card Number: 74-15626

 MENTOR TRADEMARK REG. U.S. PAT. OFF. AND FOREIGN COUNTRIES
REGISTERED TRADEMARK—MARCA REGISTRADA
HECHO EN CHICAGO, U.S.A.

SIGNET, SIGNET CLASSICS, MENTOR, PLUME, MERIDIAN AND NAL
BOOKS are published *in the United States* by
The New American Library, Inc.,
1633 Broadway, New York, New York 10019,
in Canada by The New American Library of Canada Limited,
81 Mack Avenue, Scarborough, Ontario M1L 1M8,
in the United Kingdom by The New English Library Limited,
Barnard's Inn, Holborn, London, EC1N 2JR, England.

FIRST PRINTING, JANUARY, 1975

3 4 5 6 7 8 9 10 11

PRINTED IN THE UNITED STATES OF AMERICA

Contents

Preface

Writing even a short book about behavioral psychology presents problems not encountered in writing such a book about, say, Freudian or Jungian psychology. The latter are wholly defined systems invented by the men whose names they bear, and even later elaborations of followers are consonant with original views and aims. So summary and commentary would be the chief tasks of the author.

Not so with behavioral psychology. Although in the USSR the work of Pavlov dominates behavioral theory and practice, the scene in this country is more varied. True, all behavioral psychologists share certain assumptions; but once this is said, one must acknowledge that on close viewing the number of precise points of agreement is limited. The picture one gets from the twin viewpoints of the history of behavioral psychology and of its contemporary presence is one of a science unfinished and in process. This is both good and bad. It is good in the sense that no dead hand of a pioneer or founder restricts inquiry to certain fixed formulations. It is bad in that behavioral psychology presents an imprecise image, which cannot be sharpened without peril to the truth.

In putting this book together, the author has relied to a considerable degree on secondary sources which cover some aspects, or represent particular views, of behavioral psychology but not others. All sources, primary and secondary, are given chapter for chapter in the notes at the back. Though summary and commentary comprise a substantial part of the writing, its main thrust is toward condensation and synthesis, although a synthesis which, for reasons already stated, must remain incomplete.

That aspects of behavioral psychology, both in its experimental and therapeutic phases, have been slighted will be recognized by anyone familiar with the subject. However, the book is intended primarily to give an overview to the uninitiated. In this regard, the author has been mindful of Ben Jonson's figurative maxim for teaching: in transferring wine from large into small bottles, pour a little and slowly, lest most of the beverage be spilled.

What I have referred to as the imprecise image of behavioral psychology has occasioned all kinds of charges against it—including the most serious one that it is totalitarian and fascistic. Because it tends to view human behavior as lawful and limited, because it believes that behavior can be managed and controlled, and because it takes small account of individual idiosyncrasy, certain critics have depicted behavioral psychology as dangerous to freedom and as presaging George Orwell's *1984*. But Perry London has pointed out: "The idea that behavior is lawful is . . . the most elementary axiom in the scientist's creed and . . . also common to much of the theology of Judaism and Christianity." And as B. F. Skinner has shown, a great deal of what passes for freedom is simply an *unawareness* of management. Aware or not, each of us responds continually to the stimuli of an environment that accepts and rewards some kinds of behavior and discourages and punishes other kinds. A science that might help us to build a world in which man's actions bring him greater happiness, peace, and satisfaction is scarcely to be shunned.

A. B.

Part One:

INTRODUCTION

These circuitous ways to death [are] . . . neither more nor less than the phenomena of life as we know it . . . the whole life of instinct serves the one end of bringing about death.

FREUD (1948)

All life is nothing other than the realization of one purpose, *viz.*, the preservation of life itself, the tireless labor of which may be called the general *instinct of life*.

PAVLOV (1928)

Chapter One

Two Approaches

Psychodynamic and Behavioral Psychology

Of the two main approaches to psychology—the psychodynamic and the behavioral—the former clearly dominated the first half of the twentieth century, and only in the last decade or two has a broad interest in the latter appeared. The reasons for both of these phenomena are various. Psychodynamic psychology, particularly as exemplified by Sigmund Freud and his followers, had an intensely liberating effect on the post-Victorian mind. It not only peeled away the outer layers of a rigid and suffocating public morality to reveal a complex, seething private world of hidden conflicts and desires, it provided a justification and rationale for doing so. The way people behaved, said Freud, was not just the result of what they consciously thought or willed but also of deeply buried feelings and wishes. Experienced in the early years of life but frowned on or forbidden by civilized society, these feelings and wishes were denied. But they remained operative in the unconscious—rising, uncalled-for, symbolically in dreams, free associations, and seemingly irrational actions. Behavioral problems, then, were not really problems as such but symptoms of hidden disorders caused by the repressed material. Only when these disorders—called neuroses, psychoses, and psychoneuroses—were unearthed, analyzed, and their components understood and dealt with by the individual would the problems effectively disappear.

The famous case of Little Hans illustrates the Freudian psychodynamic approach. Hans was a five-year-old boy with an intense fear of horses who was brought to Freud. Although the boy's history revealed a number of bad experiences with horses, Freud was convinced by the severity of the phobia that these experiences had not produced the condition. In Freud's view, the phobia displaced a more deep-seated dread of the child's father, whose rivalry for the mother gave rise to guilt and danger, according to the Oedipal model. Attacking the boy's manifest fear of horses would not have relieved the real cause of the anxiety even if it eliminated the phobia; it would have left untouched the central problem, and a new defense against anxiety would have risen in place of the old one. The phobia, like all problem behavior, was only the tip of a psychic iceberg, the true dimensions of which could be gauged only with patient probing and a knowledge equal to the cunning of the unconscious mind. In short, with the methods of psychoanalysis—by which Hans was cured.

This unwillingness to accept the obvious as the truth, combined with a creative and insightful curiosity about the processes of the mind, brought psychodynamic psychology perhaps its greatest esteem. Not only in the hospital and the consulting room, but in literature, the arts, and culture generally the influence of psychodynamic psychology came to be widely felt. It offered a new way of looking at man and his behavior, it showed man to be infinitely more complex, ingenious, and interesting than had before been supposed; it seemed to unlock ancient mysteries of "personality."

By comparison, behavioral psychology seemed a humdrum affair, a matter of professors in laboratories watching rats go through mazes, testing the responses of animals and people to all manner of stimuli, keeping records heavy with statistics. It offered no constructs of the mind equal in daring and invention to Freud's—or

Jung's or Reich's or other psychodynamic psychologists. In fact, it largely ignored the mind. It confined itself to the obvious: it confined itself to observable behavior. What the psychodynamic school considered merely symptomatic, the tip of the iceberg, the behavioral school thought worth studying, in fact it thought the *only* thing worth studying. It viewed man not as some restless inner swirl of conflicts, dramas, dreams, and hidden secrets, but as an animal scarcely different from other vertebrates, responding to stimuli in ways similar to theirs, and so to be studied. The behavioral psychologists acknowledged that man had a mind—so, for that matter, did animals—but they considered it unimportant. For one thing, what went on in the mind was subjective and couldn't be examined scientifically. But more essentially, states of feeling, thoughts, fantasies were secondary to actual aspects of behavior, which were traceable to specific stimuli and accorded with discoverable laws.

Obviously, such an approach to psychology had little appeal to the popular imagination. The collection and testing of minute data in the laboratory is seldom stirring, even to the collectors themselves. Pavlov's experiments with dogs, in which the animals were conditioned to salivate at the ringing of a bell, had excited a certain public interest, but the ramifications of these experiments still seemed limited to most.

Nevertheless the work went on; and then, beginning in the 1950s, a certain dissatisfaction with psychodynamic psychology began to set in, and an increasing criticism both of its methodology and its results started to be heard. In 1952 H. J. Eysenck of the University of London published his famous review of psychodynamic therapy in which he showed that the remission rate in treated neurotics was much the same as the spontaneous recovery rate of untreated neurotics. The implications of this study—as well as of the subsequent debate which has centered around psychotherapy—are more complicated than would appear. Eysenck alleged that he did not wish to put down his fellow psychiatrists and psychoanalysts but to goad them into using better controls. Nevertheless, the effect was to place in further doubt a psychology which until only a few years before had seemed millennial.

The search for a more reliable therapy dates from this time, and now attention began to be paid to the behaviorists. Behavioral psychology was nothing new—its development dates from the late nineteenth century—but it had worked out in the laboratory a variety of behavior modification procedures that could be applied to patients with behavior problems with impressive results.

Here is an example.

As early as 1924, in an almost precise counterpart of Freud's case of Little Hans, Mary Cover Jones applied behavioral methods in the treatment of a boy named Peter who also had an animal phobia. Little Peter, age two, was frightened by rabbits, white rats, and even furs and cotton wool. Discounting the possible psychic influence of the child's Oedipal father, Jones applied a classic conditioning program. While Peter was happily engaged in playing with three other children, she introduced a rabbit. This was done day after day. At first, the boy's responsive fear continued strong, but gradually, as the sessions went on, it began to abate, and Peter would tolerate the animal being brought closer and closer. By the forty-fifth session, he was able to take the rabbit in his arms and fondle it, while the gentle creature nibbled his fingers.

Here is another example.

In 1938 O. H. and W. M. Mowrer reported on their experiments with children who were bed wetters. Again ignoring Freudian and other psychodynamic models, the Mowrers thought the problem, called enuresis, might ensue from failure of the sleeping child to respond to the cues of a full bladder. If a device would be found to awaken the child to become alert to his bladder tension, the child would inhibit urination until he got to the bathroom.

Like Pavlov, the Mowrers selected a bell as the stimulus. They equipped the child's bed with a pad containing wires in a broken circuit. When the sleeping child emitted only a little bit of urine, the electrolytic properties of the liquid completed the circuit and the bell rang, stimulating the reflex response of awakening. Gradually, the use of this apparatus could be withdrawn as the child learned to respond to the bladder stimulus. In experiments with this conditioning device on thirty children, the Mowrers were able to report cures in every case.

Little Hans or Little Peter? The problems of human behavior are unfortunately too complex and far-reaching for such a simplistic formula. Many of the principles of psychodynamic psychology continue to be upheld in practice, while among behavioral psychologists, as we shall see, there are numerous differences about methods and goals. But that behavioral psychology has come into its own in our day cannot be disputed. And just as the rise of Freudian psychology—despite its merits—was related to a cultural need for release from Victorian moral oppressiveness, the "discovery" of behavioral psychology, despite its merits, fits in with certain cultural aspects of the present—particularly the tendency to see human behavior in the model of machines, as a system in which signals are fed in and other signals are given out. This too is a simplification, and the most sensitive and advanced behavioral psychologists have already gone beyond it.

Part Two:

THEORIES OF

BEHAVIOR

The world of the mind steals the show. Behavior is not recognized as a subject in its own right. In psychotherapy, for example, the disturbing things a person does or says are almost always regarded merely as symptoms, and compared with the fascinating dramas which are staged in the depths of the mind, behavior itself seems superficial indeed. In linguistics and literary criticism what a man says is almost always treated as the expression of ideas or feelings . . . . For more than twenty-five hundred years close attention has been paid to mental life, but only recently has any effort been made to study human behavior as something more than a mere by-product.

B. F. Skinner (1971)

Chapter Two

Behavior and Contiguity

Sechenev, Pavlov, Watson, Guthrie

Although behavioral psychology as a science is largely a creation of the last hundred years, its principles of learning and its techniques of behavior modification are as old as the records of man. The Hebrews', and later the Puritans', prohibition of graven images sprang from the idea of an invisible God, but it also entailed removal of stimuli to idol worship. In his *Natural History,* Pliny the Elder described a variety of aversive behavioral methods for curing alcoholism, ranging from physical and social punishment to the placing of spiders in the bottom of the tippler's winecup. An early nineteenth-century physician, Johan Reil, treated severely melancholic and torpid patients by infesting them with scabies; the resultant itching presumably reinforced motor activity. And James Ward in a discussion of ideation in the 1870s seemingly took note of the conditioned reflex before Pavlov when he observed that "the dog's mouth waters at the sight of food, but the gourmand's mouth will water at the thought of it."

But such isolated observations and experiments, which might be multiplied a thousandfold, only forecast the *science* of behavioral psychology, whose history properly begins with the work of Sechenev.

Ivan M. Sechenev (1829–1904) is one of those scientific giants whose contributions to knowledge are absorbed and superseded by later figures and whose due place in science history is rarely, if ever, afterwards acknowledged. The first student of behavior "to replace philosophical deliberation and incidental observation with rigorous experimentation," Sechenev was born in Russia, where he received his early training in physiology, and then studied abroad with Claude Bernard and Herman von Helmholtz. He taught at the St. Petersburg Military Medical Academy and later at Moscow University.

While experimenting on the inhibition of reflex movements by the cerebral cortex, Sechenev became convinced that there was a purely physiological basis for mental activity. This he set out to discover and explain. The main obstacle in his path was the traditional distinction between involuntary and so-called voluntary behavior.

That certain simple acts, the blinking of the eyes in response to a strong light, the withdrawal of the hand from contact with extreme heat, were involuntary and reflexive was generally acknowledged. But conventional wisdom held that other, more complicated acts originated in the mind. Sechenev disagreed; "*all* animal and human acts are reflex in essence," he said. Even man's highest artistic and intellectual achievements can be seen as "associations . . . effected through series of contacts between consecutive reflexes." It is interesting to note that these assertions were published in 1863.

Sechenev attacked the problem as a misunderstanding of neurological development which needed to be clarified. The human infant has only a limited sensory capacity because it has not learned to use its musculature in response to stimuli; it is also limited in the variety of its reflexes, which tend to be elicited en masse.

On seeing a brightly colored object, for instance, the baby tends to follow it with its eyes, to the exclusion of other objects which give it less pleasure. Moreover, the child "screams, laughs, moves its arms, legs and body; it is clear," says Sechenev, "that the child is capable of reflexes from the optical nerve in all the animal muscles of the body."

Thus a simple stimulus—the brightly colored object

—leads to a complex set of cross-modal associations in which visual, tactile, and kinesthetic stimuli and responses all become associated. Other stimuli—food, mother, mother with food, mother with food and brightly colored object—elicit other sets of associations. Over the years, the development, refinement, and integration of such associations as the child grows up end with the acquisition of adult capabilities.

Starting with the baby's delight at the brightly colored object, emotional reactions also are affected by association, and shift from one stimulus to another—from the object itself to the mother conveying it and also to other brightly colored things: a knight in a story book, the child's own clothing, and so on to the highest forms of human perception. But the emotions are also subject to a second law: repeated stimulation tends to dull emotional response. So the child becomes weary of brightly colored objects, the youth loses interest in his games, the lover tires of his love, etc. Other factors tend to inhibit emotional reflexes, as when the parent admonishes the child with the consequences of an action: if you do such and such, such and such else will happen.

All reflexes, according to Sechenev, are subject to inhibition, and in this connection he defined the role of thought. Thought is "the first two thirds of a reflex." Where inhibition occurs, the initial and central components of a reflex take place, but the final one—overt behavior—is missing. Put another way, thought is no more than an inhibited reflex.

Beyond this limited role, human thinking, as it is conceived in the notion of voluntary behavior, is a fiction. To account for the prevalence of the idea of behavior independent of reflexes, Sechenev posited the ego. Through the development of his ego, man comes to believe that certain of his actions are willed; but this is wrong, an illusion, a chimera of thought. "All psychical acts without exception . . . are developed by means of reflexes. Hence, all conscious movements (usually called voluntary), inasmuch as they arise from these acts, are reflex, in the strictest sense of the word."

In his view of abnormal behavior, Sechenev approached, but did not recognize, the phenomenon of conditioning: where associations are misdirected or confused, inappropriate or undesirable behavior will occur. In this respect, Sechenev leads to Pavlov, who in many ways was influenced by Sechenev and his work.

Ivan Petrovich Pavlov (1849–1936) was the son of a village priest and was educated at the local seminary. He then studied at the University of St. Petersburg, where he specialized in animal physiology. After receiving his degree in 1875 he became an advanced student of physiology in the medical school, and then, like Sechenev, went abroad to study with the leading physiologists of the day.

Like Sechenev he taught at the St. Petersburg Military Medical Academy—but here the resemblance in careers varies for a time. Pavlov devoted himself entirely to research on digestion; it is for this that he received the Nobel Prize in 1904. He was fifty years old when, somewhat reluctantly, he left his work on digestion and began to study the phenomena of conditioning, with which his name would afterwards be linked.

This is how it came about. In order to study the digestive glands of dogs, Pavlov had developed surgical techniques by which the animal's secretions could be brought to the surface for collection, measurement, and analysis. In the course of his experiments, Pavlov noticed that his dogs secreted saliva even before food was given to them—not only on seeing the food but also on hearing the footfalls of laboratory assistants.

What had occurred, of course, was *classical conditioning*: the animals responded to stimuli associated with eating with the same reflexive behavior that occurred at the actual ingestion of the food.

Pavlov struggled with the question of whether to pursue this line of observation further. He knew that he would meet with disapproval from his fellow physiologists for diverting his research from the physical to the mental, psychology then being held in some dis-esteem.

Yet Sechenev had set an example that was not to be deprecated. In the end, Pavlov decided to proceed.

Still there is a certain defensiveness in the rigor of his statements of the time, which seem to reflect an ongoing struggle. Thus in 1903 he declared: "Vital phenomena that are termed psychic are distinguishable from pure physiological phenomena only in degree of complexity. Whether we call these phenomena psychical or complex nervous is of little importance, as long as it is . . . recognized that the naturalist approaches them and studies them only objectively. . . ."

In his 1906 Thomas Huxley Lecture the tone is similar: "The naturalist has no right to speak of higher animals' psychic processes without deserting the principles of natural science—which is the work of the human mind directed to nature through studies that derive their assumptions and interpretations from no other source than external nature itself." That there might be a contradiction between his reference to the human mind and the rest of the statement seems to have eluded Pavlov at the time.

In any case, Pavlov's work followed the simple model he had first observed. Two kinds of stimuli were presented: the one that naturally elicited the reflex, which he called the *unconditioned stimulus,* and another that accompanied it and eventually could be made to elicit the response by itself. The latter *conditioned stimulus* might be practically anything. Pavlov preferred to use a bell, a tuning fork, or a light flash, all of which could be made to cause a dog's saliva to flow.

In theoretical terms, "Pavlov's concept of the ultimate nature of conditioning," says Kimble, "was that the intense (*dominant*) activity (excitation) set up in one neural center by the unconditioned stimulus (US) attracted to itself the weaker activity (excitation) initiated by other stimuli present at approximately the same time. Later on, he postulated that the activity in these two centers *irradiated* and met somewhere in between the two centers."

An important aspect of conditioning is that it is temporary. Pavlov actually used the word "conditional" in his writings to suggest this; "condition*ed*"—which may imply something permanent—is a mistranslation that later writers, including the present one, have perpetuated. Still, the difference is not very large to anyone who understands how conditioning occurs.

The conditional nature of the conditioned response is shown in the phenomenon of *extinction*. Pavlov found that an animal's response to the conditioned stimulus, if not reinforced by re-presentation of the unconditioned stimulus, tends to disappear. Thus Pavlov's dogs, which learned to salivate at the ringing of a bell, would stop salivating on the presentation of this conditioned stimulus after a time unless meat powder was periodically placed on their tongues. But under certain conditions, Pavlov found, conditioned responses could lose their strength even when they were so reinforced. "He considered that the reason for this loss of effectiveness was that the conditioned responses after a considerable amount of practice passed into a state of inhibition. The growth of this type of inhibition was facilitated when the conditioned stimuli were applied at short intervals of time. . . ."

Just as conditioning was not always permanent, so extinction might not be. An animal's reflexive response to a conditioned stimulus might be extinguished and then be elicited again, even without reinforcement, if time were allowed for the reflex to rest. This return of the conditioned response is called *spontaneous recovery*.

Conditioned responses, Pavlov discovered, could serve as unconditioned responses, once they were learned, to produce *secondary conditioning*. If a dog salivated upon the placement of meat powder on his tongue while a bell tinkled, he could learn to salivate on the ringing of the bell while a colored square was presented, and then he could learn to salivate at the sight of the colored square alone. Secondary conditioning might go on to third-order conditioning, but then could go no further.

Pavlov also studied *generalization* and *discrimination*.

Generalization is the tendency of a variety of similar stimuli to induce the conditioned response. For example, a sound of a certain pitch is originally used to elicit the reflex of salivation; and then sounds of higher and lower pitch are used to accomplish the same purpose. The range of pitches at which salivation occurs is the extent of the process of generalization.

However, there are limits to this phenomenon. Sounds of a pitch that is too high or too low will not induce the response. This ability of the organism to filter out inappropriate stimuli is called discrimination.

The range of generalization can be narrowed, or the degree of discrimination sharpened, by further training. Say the dog is given food while a sound of a certain pitch is presented and is not given the food when another sound is presented; the animal will learn to salivate on hearing the one sound but not the other. But there are certain limits to the dog's ability to discriminate. The sounds must be sufficiently far apart in range; if they are too similar, discrimination will become confused. "In this connection, Pavlov discovered that some dogs, pushed beyond their limits of discrimination, break down, lose whatever discriminatory ability they have already gained, and become agitated." Observations of this kind led Pavlov into the field of abnormal psychology, in which he experimented with and studied conditions that induce neurosis.

These conditions, he said, were of five types, all involving excessive activity in the processes of excitation or inhibition. Besides tasks of conditioned discrimination, which were too difficult for his animals to perform, Pavlov found that neurotic behavior could be induced by physical stress; using intense stimuli; increasing the time between presentation of the signal and the food; and continually alternating positive and negative stimuli in a conditioning task.

Pavlov observed that some dogs did not respond to conditioning tasks in the same fashion as others, and this led him to classify his animals according to their reactivity; later he so classified humans. Here, and in his projection of the causes of animal breakdowns onto man, Pavlov sometimes overstepped the limits of empirical inquiry and entered the realm of speculation.

In his later years, many of his greatest discoveries behind him, Pavlov relaxed his strict behaviorist stance. "Certainly psychology in so far as it deals with the subjective state of man," he wrote in 1924, "has a natural right to existence; our subjective world is the first reality with which we are confronted." And four years later he criticized a fellow scientist who had experimented with conditioned bulb-pressing by schoolchildren for not getting the children's subjective reports.

"Human subjects, not being dogs, should be questioned about the conditioning experiments they undergo. . . . My earlier practice of not using subjective terms in order to avoid conceptual confusion is now, with full development of our field, valid only for younger co-workers."

The legacy of Pavlov's work—the full range of which has only been suggested here—became the foundation of most behavioral inquiry in the United States as well as in the USSR. One feature of this work must not go unnoted. Pavlov already had extensive research facilities when he began his experiments in conditioning. When the Soviets came to power, these facilities were expanded, and a growing number of associates and assistants joined him—some two hundred over the years. The work they did was coordinated and programatic, and in its mass represented an achievement of government-sponsored pure research whose like had not been seen before.

Within the same year that Pavlov switched the focus of his studies from digestion to conditioning, John Broadus Watson (1878–1958) received the first Ph.D. in psychology granted by the University of Chicago. He was then twenty-two years old.

He had written his doctoral dissertation on the learning of rats in mazes and did much research with animals afterward. His observations of their behavior *as* behavior led him to question why human behavior was not studied in the same way—objectively and without reference to consciousness and its unreliable introspective data.

At the beginning of the century, American psychology abounded with half-baked mentalistic notions. One of these was that individuals are born with certain traits, proclivities, and abilities which remain constant or determinative all their lives. Another was the theory that motivation was reducible to certain instincts, so that, for instance, quarreling came from an instinct of pugnacity, kindness from an instinct of affection, and so on. To all this, Watson said, Nonsense.

In 1913, he published what was in effect the manifesto of a new American psychology:

"Psychology as the behaviorist views it is a purely objective branch of natural science. His theoretical goal is the prediction and control of behavior. Introspection forms no essential part of its methods, nor is the scientific value of its data dependent upon the readiness with which they lend themselves to interpretation in terms of consciousness."

If this sounds like Sechenev and Pavlov, the resemblance is more one of coincidence than of direct influence. Watson came to Pavlov only after he had independently drawn the main lines of his system, and he would be unable to read Sechenev in English translation for two more decades. Indeed, the development of a purely physical psychology was an inevitable concomitant of the evolution of other physical sciences which had freed themselves of mentalistic and religious ideas, and we should not be surprised that it occurred in more than one place.

Watson regarded all behavior as learned by classic conditioning. Man is born with certain simple, demonstrable reflexes which constitute the whole of his behavioral inheritance. Gradually, as he matures, he learns to make responses to stimuli paired with the original stimulus which alone elicited them. Complex learning, such as walking, constitutes an interconnected series of conditioned reflex movements in which each movment serves as the conditioned stimulus for the movement that follows it. Thus the initial stimulus for walking may be a view of a desirable place. The first leg is swung forward, then the other, but the intricacy of the operation is greater than it appears. As Winfred Hill explains:

> . . . the person can swing his leg forward only if his weight is on the other foot. Hence, whenever he swings his leg forward, he does so in the presence of those sensations from his own body that result from having his weight on the other foot. Those sensations thus are paired with the response of swinging the leg, and through repeated pairings they come to elicit leg swinging. Hence, in the well-learned habit of walking, the sensation of having weight on one foot automatically elicits the conditioned response of swinging the other leg forward. This response merges with the others in the sequence, each providing the stimulus for the next response. The sequence eventually becomes so well integrated that for practical purposes we can speak of the whole process of walking from one place to another as a single response . . . .

Complex learning occurs in relation to two laws, that of *frequency* and that of *recency*. Watson held that the more frequently a given response is made to a given stimulus, the more likely that response is to occur again to that stimulus. And the more recently a given response is made to a given stimulus, the more likely that response is to occur again to that stimulus. Thus the act of walking is easily executed because it is marked both by frequency and recency. But in unusual circumstances, as when one has endured a long illness in bed, knowledge of the reflex sequence fades, and the patterns of movements must be relearned before they can be carried out with their former ease and efficiency.

Is intellectual attainment also a matter of conditioned learning? Yes, said Watson. When we are asked for the square root of sixty-four and answer, "The square root of sixty-four is eight," we may attribute our response to cogitation. But our series of words which follows the series of words of our questioner is only the dominant re-

sponse in a complicated sequence of conditioned movements, among which are movements of tongue, mouth,
and vocal cords. We may also furrow our brows, pace
the floor, throw up our arms. All complex behavior—
even of the highest sort—involves movments that engage the entire body.

Although Watson abjured consciousness as an area
for exploration by the psychologist, he did recognize
three emotional reaction patterns which he labeled as
fear, rage, and love. These reaction patterns basically do
not differ, except in complexity, from ordinary reflexes.
We can observe the stimuli which induce them, and both
the internal and external movements they entail. However, Watson typically warned that when a loud gong is
struck and a child starts to cry, we may speak of the
emotion of fear *as the behavior* of the child and not as a
state of its inner feeling.

Any of the three emotional reaction patterns is subject to conditioning to new stimuli. The gong and the
child just referred to were used in a famous early conditioning experiment by Watson and Rosalie Rayner, their
report of which is one of the most interesting items in
behavioral literature.*

The child, Albert B., "was reared almost from birth
in a hospital environment; his mother was a wet nurse in
the Harriet Lane Home for Invalid Children. Albert's
life was normal: he was healthy from birth and one of
the best developed youngsters ever brought to the hospital, weighing twenty-one pounds at nine months of age.
He was on the whole stolid and unemotional."

Watson and Rayner ran stolid, unemotional Albert
through a series of tests designed to elicit fear reactions.
Specifically, Albert was successively confronted with "a
white rat, a rabbit, a dog, a monkey, with masks with
and without hair, cotton wool, burning newspapers,
etc. . . . *At no time did this infant ever show fear in*

* A further discussion of this experiment and its significance
will be found at the beginning of Chapter Five.

any situation." Finally the authors introduced the loud gong. The child soon broke into a fit of crying.

So classic conditioning was undertaken with the objective of inducing a fear reaction with the previously harmless white rat, by pairing the stimulus of the animal with the stimulus of the gong. After about three and a half months of such conditioning sessions, not only did Albert show fear of the white rat, but the reaction had generalized so that a Santa Claus mask, a fur coat, a dog, and a rabbit caused him to whimper or cry.

And then before poor little Albert could be reconditioned—one of the ways Watson and Rayner had thought to do this was by pairing the fear-inducing stimuli with erogenous stimulation—Albert's mother snatched him out of the hospital. Enough was enough —if not too much.

At the end of their report, Watson and Rayner speculate on Albert's future:

"The Freudians twenty years from now, unless their hypotheses change, when they come to analyze Albert's fear of a sealskin coat—assuming that he comes to analysis at that age—will probably tease from him the recital of a dream which upon their analysis will show that Albert at three years of age attempted to play with the pubic hair of the mother and was scolded violently for it."

This offhandedness was too often a characteristic of Watson's approach. If he was successful in lampooning systems of psychology that did not accord with his objective standards, he was less so in fully working out his own theories. His occasional inconsistency and lack of thoroughness have been commented on by more than one critic. Had he stuck to his work, he might have obviated these objections. As it was, by the 1920s Watson moved completely out of the field of experimental psychology—and finished his career as an advertising executive!

But Watson's enormous contribution is indisputable: he laid down a body of basic theory and set the direction in which American psychology would afterwards go. His belief that all men are equal, in that they are born with nothing more than the same conditionable reflexes, fits well with democratic ideals. The idea that everything we are is learned, and its corollary, that everything we have learned can be unlearned was consonant both with America's faith in education and its optimistic temper. In time the central focus of learning in Watson's system, and the systems of the other men who followed and in many ways superseded him, gave behavioral psychology the alternative name of *learning theory*.*

One of the most important of these men was Edwin R. Guthrie, who taught at the University of Washington from 1914 until his retirement in 1956.

Guthrie is unique among psychologists in that his education was in philosophy. Throughout his life he retained the philosopher's bent for reducing complex phenomena to simple principles, and his examples were as often taken from life as from the laboratory.

Like Watson, learning was for Guthrie a matter of conditioning, but he stated the case in a far more general way: "A combination of stimuli which has accompanied a movement will on its recurrence tend to be followed by that movement." This rule, which resembles Watson's law of recency (Guthrie rejected the law of frequency), is the basic tenet of Guthrian psychology.

Certain objections to the simplicity of this rule will immediately occur.

Guthrie says nothing about the pairing of unconditioned and conditioned stimuli by which response to the latter is induced. On the other hand, he does not deny the fact of classical conditioning either. Whether the response is elicited through training or in some other manner, it will tend to be repeated in the presence of the same stimuli.

---

* The term "behavioral psychology" has also been used to include nonlearning techniques that affect behavior, such as the use of drugs and chemicals. The definition of a term is what one makes it, I suppose. In this book, learning theory and behavioral psychology are strictly interchangeable.

But what about a situation in which a multiplicity of stimuli and responses occur; which response is most likely to occur the next time? The last one, says Guthrie.

If a person is given a mechanical puzzle to solve and he solves it, the next time he is given the puzzle, he will solve it again; and we say that he has learned to do the puzzle. But if he has not solved the puzzle and merely pushed it away the first time, he is also likely to give up on the task in the same manner on a succeeding try. From an objective view, learning has occurred here too. In both instances the person has learned to deal with, by removing, the stimulus of the unsolved puzzle, and the particular response he made the first time will probably be the one he makes the next. That we label one response successful and the other unsuccessful is irrelevant; both responses equally represent the same principle of *contiguous conditioning.*

Guthrie's lack of concern with reward, or reinforcement, raises still other objections, but in this regard he continues to stand his ground firmly. Any given response to a given situation depends on whether that response changes that situation to another situation. The solving of the puzzle changes the situation which contained the unsolved puzzle, but so does pushing the puzzle away. Both behaviors remove the problem and in that sense are self-reinforcing and likely to recur. Inefficient methods are acquired and retained, just as efficient ones are, and are equally likely to be repeated. Learning occurs not because particular responses are rewarded or punished, but simply because they have been made.

If Guthrie does not admit reinforcement, how then does he explain extinction? Easily; extinction is learning to replace one response with another.

If a particular response changes a situation so that it is repeated, and then it no longer changes the situation, new responses will be tried. Then the last response made will tend to replace the original one and be repeated when the situation is presented anew, and the original response will tend to die out.

Suppose a cat has learned to get out of a box by opening a flap in the side, and then that flap is closed up. It will learn to get out by pushing a flap on the top, and the new response will gradually replace the old one, which will grow weaker. Now, if the box is totally sealed up so that the cat cannot get out in any way, after a great many fits and starts, mewings and scratchings, the cat will change its situation by curling up and closing its eyes, until it is freed from the box by a friendly human. The next time the cat is placed in the box it will be more likely to repeat its most recent response than the two earlier responses, which have been extinguished, as long as the stimulus situation does not change.

Guthrie acknowledged the complexity of the stimulus situation, which he said included not only the cues arising from inside the box but also the cues emanating from inside the cat. This seems to be the basis for his stating his rule in terms of probability or tendency. If the cat experienced a sudden gas pain, for instance, this would be part of one stimulus situation but perhaps not of another. In more general terms, the stimulus situation as perceived by the animal varies from trial to trial, so that the animal is conditioned by practice to respond to more and more of the stimuli that may occur in the total situation.

Allowing for such variables—some might call them loopholes—Guthrie was able to account for all manner of behavior. Habits, for instance. These, like other movements, follow the principles of contiguity and recurrence. A bad habit is simply an undesirable response to a stimulus situation which is repeated each time the situation is presented. A good habit is no different, except that the response is desirable; it is as likely to re-occur as the undesirable response if it is learned to alter the stimulus situation.

Guthrie illustrates this with an example of a ten-year-old girl who threw her hat and coat on the floor each time she entered the house. Each time her mother scolded her, but each time the action was repeated. Finally, her mother made her put on the hat and coat, go out the door, come in again, and then hang up her clothes. After this had happened a few times, the little girl learned to hang her clothing up without throwing it down first. The last (desirable) response had gained in dominance over the earlier (undesirable) one, just for being the last action the girl performed to change the situation. What the mother's scolding had failed to accomplish, contiguous conditioning was able to achieve.

In another example, Guthrie tells about another little girl who was in the habit of lighting matches. Again the mother's scolding did no good. (Guthrie, like other learning theorists—notably Hull and Skinner, as we shall presently see—had scant regard for punishment as an instrument of learning.) So the mother sat the little girl down with a box of matches and told her to light one match after another. Even after the child grew tired of the game, her mother insisted that she go on lighting matches. At last the little girl threw the box of matches down and kicked it away. This being her last response to the stimulus of the matchbox, it was likely to be made the next time. And indeed, Guthrie tells us, the little girl thereafter avoided matchboxes as much as she had been attracted to them before.

Both examples illustrate Guthrie's law. But they illustrate other things as well. The little girl who threw her hat and coat on the floor experienced a cessation of her mother's scolding (negative reinforcement) and, we can imagine, received praise (positive reinforcement) when she switched to hanging the garments up. The little girl who grew tired of lighting matches experienced a severe inhibition of her match-lighting response through its repeated practice, in accordance with Pavlovian—and Hullian—findings.* And the replacement of one habit with another in both cases is less satisfactorily explained by the principle of recency than by that of the reciprocal inhibition of one response habit by another.†

---

* Hull's theory of inhibition is summarized in the next chapter.
† See Chapter Six for a full discussion of reciprocal inhibition.

And yet Guthrie's law does explain the cases of both little girls. There is, in fact, hardly any area of behavior to which the law does not apply. Take forgetting: it is simply the reverse side of learning. An old habit of response—whether it involves language or a physical skill —is lost because a new one has taken its place.

So Guthrie always seems to have the last word. His net is so wide that it gathers in everything, and whatever slips through does not contradict him. Is he profoundly simple or simply incomplete? Discussion of Guthrie's system must eventually come to grips with this most unpsychological of problems. There is something very attractive about a theory that rests on a single rule, but when it involves a matter as complex as human behavior there is also something disturbing about it too.

As Hilgard and Bower say:

> One of the sources of uneasiness about Guthrie's system lies in its assured answers to the problems of learning— answers that remained unchanged through more than a quarter century of the most active psychological experimentation we have ever known. Experimental controversies finally get resolved as we learn more about the independent variables that modify the measured consequences. No matter how these issues get resolved, Guthrie's system remains unchanged. Either the theory is a miraculously inspired one or it is not stated very precisely, and hence is not very sensitive to experimental data.

But even here Guthrie has the last word: "The principle of association or conditioning is not an explanation of any instance of behavior. It is merely a tool by which explanation is futhered. A tool is not true or false; it is useful."

The theories of behavior of Sechenev, Pavlov, Watson, and Guthrie share one characteristic. They are all built on the principle of association or contiguity. Stimulus leads to response without reference to reinforcement or reward. Pavlov did apply reinforcement to the limited extent of using the unconditioned stimulus to

strengthen the conditioned one. But he does not otherwise belong with the learning theorists we shall consider
in the next chapter, to whom reinforcement is a central
factor in determining what men and animals do.

Chapter Three

Behavior and Reinforcement

Thorndike, Hull, Skinner

First of the reinforcement theorists, Edward L. Thorndike (1874–1949), taught at Columbia University Teachers College from 1899 until his retirement some forty years later. Like Watson, he did his early work with animals, and his *Animal Intelligence,* published when he was thirty-one, made his reputation. The book comprised his doctoral dissertation plus articles on his subsequent experiments.

One of these experiments involved a cat in a cage. The cage had a door that could be opened by pulling a looped string. Outside the door was a piece of fish.

Presented with this situation, the cat at first walked around, scratching at the walls of the cage, before it pulled the string and got out. Gradually the interval between its placement in the cage and its opening the door grew shorter. But even after going through several drills, the cat still spent a good deal of time performing other actions before it pulled the string. Thorndike therefore concluded that the cat did not rationally infer a relationship between the door opening and its pulling the string but that there was a gradual *stamping-in* of the string-pulling response to the stimulus of the string.

Now this is still consistent with the theories of Watson

and Guthrie; where Thorndike parted company with the contiguity theorists was in calling attention to the fish tidbit as a factor governing the stimulus-response connection. If this reward was instrumental in affecting the cat's behavior, the conditioning involved was different from classical conditioning, which depends solely on stimulus-pairing. This different kind of conditioning, which entails behavior leading to reward or escape from punishment, is called *instrumental conditioning*. Thorndike generalized its action in a law:

> Of several responses made to the same situation, those which are accompanied or closely followed by satisfaction to the animal will, other things being equal, be more firmly connected with the situation, so that, when it recurs, they will be more likely to recur; those which are accompanied or closely followed by discomfort to the animal will, other things being equal, have their connections with that situation weakened, so that, when it recurs, they will be less likely to recur. The greater the satisfaction or discomfort, the greater the strengthening or weakening of the bond.

Thorndike called this principle the *law of effect*. Although he would postulate other laws in his long career, the law of effect became as central to his theory of behavior as Guthrie's single law was to his.

Critics attacked the law of effect for its use of such subjective terms as "satisfaction" and "discomfort," although Thorndike had been careful to give these words behavioral definitions. "By a satisfying state of affairs," he said, "is meant one which the animal does nothing to avoid, often doing such things as attain and preserve it. By a discomforting or annoying state of affairs is meant one which the animal commonly avoids and abandons." Fair enough.

But more seriously objectionable was the phrase, "other things being equal." This innocuous modifier, as one critic of Thorndike has complained, "made the theory indeterminate . . . and to a large extent incapable of disproof. . . ."

Thorndike tried to anticipate such strictures by specifying the "things"; they were three.

The first, "the frequency, energy and duration of the connection," was perhaps to some extent measurable.

The second, "the readiness of the response to be connected with the situation," is also to a degree observable. For instance, a cat is more likely to move toward a fish fillet than toward an apple, though not necessarily.

But with the third, a certain subjectivity creeps in. This was "the closeness with which the satisfaction is associated with the response, . . . most clearly seen in the effect of increasing the interval between the response and the satisfaction or discomfort." But the length or brevity of the interval between response and satisfaction was not the only consideration here. As Thorndike explains: "If a cat pushes a button around with its nose, while its main occupation, the act to which its general 'set' impels it, to which, we say, it is chiefly attentive, is that of clawing at an opening, it will be less aided in the formation of the habit than if it had been chiefly concerned in what its nose was doing."

Thorndike doesn't say that the law of effect ceases to work if the cat isn't paying attention, but only that it works better if the cat is. Still he leaves a considerable loophole in which inference and opinion can comfortably nest.

Perhaps the most serious objection to the law of effect had to do with the backward action of the reinforcement. How can a satisfaction that comes after the response cause the strengthening of a connection that has already been made?

Thorndike did not attempt to deal with this problem until 1932, some twenty-seven years after he had formulated the law. His answer was to posit a hypothetical neural mechanism which he called the "OK reaction." This mechanism, he said, zoomed back to the original stimulus-response connection to confirm and reinforce it.

Not only that: the OK reaction was capable of selecting from among several possible responses the one to be strengthened by the satisfaction. "When an animal that runs about seeking food attains it, the strengthening will be more likely to [occur with respect to] its locomotion, its hunger, and its ideas about eating, than . . . casual scatchings of an ear or stray thoughts about Shakespeare's sonnets or Brahms's symphonies."

But perhaps the most extreme change in the law was Thorndike's statement that the OK reaction was independent of sensory pleasure, and that even pain might bring about a strengthening of the stimulus-response connection.

But if pain could serve as satisfaction the self-defining quality of the law of effect was destroyed. Thorndike had, indeed, modified the law to the extent of saying that satisfactions were more important in strengthening connections, than discomforts were in weakening them. Still, according to this latest statement, anything could bring satisfaction, including its opposite.

"Clearly," Hardy Wilcoxon comments, "the Law of Effect had come upon troubled times. Otherwise its author, the foremost champion of tough-minded deterministic explanations of behavior, would never have relinquished the control of learning to an 'overhead' neural mechanism which, given the prevailing ignorance of such things at the time, could only be viewed as a 1933 model of the ancient homunculus, capable of making up its own mind."

But this criticism is not altogether fair. Though Thorndike's law of effect has largely been rejected, the principle of reinforcement it embodied has become increasingly important to behavioral psychology. Put another way, the theory did not stand up but the idea behind it did—and the experiments of Thorndike and his followers in no little way contributed to this fact.

Part of the weakness of Thorndike's position was that he tried to explain the phenomenon of reinforcement in terms that were essentially contiguist ones. He said that reinforcement was a contingency which might affect an

S-R connection, but which then again might not: there is a kind of circularity to such a formulation.

Clark L. Hull (1884–1952) theorized the principle of reinforcement in more solid terms by positing the notion of *drive*. A drive, to Hull, was any aroused state of an organism, and any stimulus that reduced a drive was reinforcing. Thus hunger is a drive which is reduced by the reinforcement of food. But a noxious situation may also function as a drive which is reducible by removal of the noxious stimulus (pain, for instance). Thus punishment does not weaken an S-R connection, its termination strengthens it. The reduction of a drive by the presentation of a stimulus is called *positive reinforcement*; the reduction of a drive by removal of a stimulus is called *negative reinforcement*.

But Hull differs from Thorndike in other ways, most notably in his overall approach. For many years a professor at Yale, Hull received his early training in engineering, and as Winfred Hill notes, "something of the engineer's outlook is evident in his desire to construct an elaborate, formal, precise structure of psychological theory."

Indeed, Hull sought to do for psychology something very much like what Newton had done for physics: establish a broad and detailed body of principles that would be applicable to the whole range of behavioral phenomena. Wilcoxon tells us that he gave Newton's *Principia*, with his own marginal notes, to his students for background reading. "The notes ('Exactly!' 'Psychology must have such laws,' etc.) . . . leave no doubt as to the source of his inspiration or of his devotion to the ideal of making psychology a deductive science."

Hull's system was highly organized but designed to be supple and capable of revision without breaking down. At its base were a series of postulates, or givens, which were used to construct theorems after the manner of geometry. These theorems were susceptible to verification and proof by experiments in the laboratory. If a theorem did not prove out under specific conditions, one or more of the postulates was in need of revision. If a theorem did prove out, this did not necessarily mean that the postulates were correct; the success of the experiment might be due to other factors, but the theorem and its components survived. Hull did not see himself as a lawgiver for all time but as a theorist who would establish a science of behavior along more concrete lines than had heretofore been laid out by any of his predecessors. He expected that psychologists who followed him would amend his construction as their experiments showed a need for changes. And in his lifetime he revised his formulations as his own experimentation demanded.

To the reader who approaches it for the first time, Hullian theory is somewhat forbidding. It is replete with numbers, strange symbols and equations which suggest the mathematical formulations of physics and chemistry more than the mythic concepts that still govern much psychological thinking. It is indeed more stirring to the imagination to contemplate the symmetry of the Oedipal triangle than an equation like $sE_R = sH_R \times D$ upon a page. Surely, one thinks intuitively, human behavior cannot be reduced to such a cut-and-dry thing, and this is partially true. Yet the particular Hullian formula we have cited has been of great use to behavior therapists in devising programs of treatment for troubled people and in verifying the results of therapy.

Let us look at the elements of the equation $sE_R = sH_R \times D$ which H. J. Eysenck considers representative of "the most important aspect of Hullian theory." E stands for performance; the subscripts s and R denote the stimulus and response which are components of the performance. H stands for habit, which also bears the stimulus-response connection, but drive, D, is independent of them. Such drives as hunger, thirst, sex, etc., have no inevitable expression in performance except as may be determined by habit. Thus a poor, hungry man may steal a chicken or beg for money to buy himself a chicken dinner to reduce his hunger, depending on which behavior is more firmly established in his repertoire. Hull's Postulate 3 states that habit strength grows with reinforcement; but according to Postulate 4 this growth lessens with each successive reinforced trial, to the point where it becomes negligible.

The distinction between habit and performance in Hull's formula constitutes an advance in definition over earlier theorists like Watson and Guthrie; and it also had a certain predictive value. If a particular habit is absent from the repertoire, a performance in accord with it will not occur, except as the inception of a new habit. But no habit in itself will guarantee performance unless drive is constant.

"When drive is zero there is no performance, however strong the habit may be; we have many habits, but these are only translated into performance when sparked off by a suitable drive. . . . It will be noted that among the variables determining the growth of habit, drive is not included. This is not an accidental oversight, but a part of the theoretical structure. For Hull the amount of drive present during learning is irrelevant."

So explains Eysenck, who goes on to declare that Hull's "paradoxical position" in this matter is not supported by more recent experimental evidence, which points to drive as having a determinative influence on the growth of habit. Here is a place where Hullian theory breaks down without losing its validity as to the basic relationship between drive, habit, and performance. The risks in creating a theory as precise and specific as Hull's, in comparison to the reductive approach of a Guthrie, are great indeed, but Hullians would argue that this is the only way of building a true science of behavior.

In his last years, Hull refined his equation for performance to include what he called *incentive motivation*. In experiments, he had observed that large rewards reduced drive more effectively than small ones and thus raised the level of performance. These rises were too spectacular to be explained by the slow growth of habit strength. Furthemore, reductions in the size of rewards resulted in poorer performances, which could not be explained by a lessening of habit strength, if the latter were to be considered a permanent bond between S and R.

The concept of incentive motivation (symbolized as K) preserved the autonomy of habit while explaining changes in performance in direct relation to magnitude of reward. In everyday language, this concept is expressed in the notion that people will work harder for high wages than for low ones. In the psychology laboratory, it is represented statistically in the increases of speed with which an animal learns to find food. A rat will gradually and progressively run faster down a channel to locate and eat a food pellet; but its speed will jump appreciably if the size of the pellet is enlarged, and fall if it is made smaller. The resultant formula, $sE_R = sH_R \times D \times K$, seems to account for these facts.

Yet even this extended formula does not tell the whole story. When a response is elicited repeatedly, the tendency of the organism to repeat it decreases, despite the presence of reinforcement. Hull termed this phenomenon, which is roughly equivalent to fatigue, *reactive inhibition,* and gave it the symbol I_R. The absence of the subscript s here expresses the fact that reactive inhibition occurs without regard to stimulus. Each time a given response occurs, the amount of I_R will increase, but then it will dissipate with rest. This explains why performance is superior when the practice of a habit is distributed so that rest periods separate individual performances.

The concept of reactive inhibition may also explain extinction, according to Hull. If performance is lowered by decreasing reinforcement, I_R will build up with successive trials until there is no further response. The dissipation of I_R with the passage of time, however, may result in and explain spontaneous recovery.

In Hull's writings we also encounter the symbol sI_R. This is related to I_R and is derived from it. Hull conceived I_R to be a negative drive which diminished with rest. However, while I_R is still strong and effective, the fact that the organism is repeatedly *not* responding to a particular stimulus makes for a habit of not responding, which is reinforced by the dissipation of I_R. This negative habit—sI_R—or *conditioned inhibition* explains why spontaneous recovery is never complete. Even with I_R absent, sI_R remains in the repertoire. Hull incorporated these two kinds of inhibition into his original formula as follows: $sE_R = (sH_R \times D) - (I_R + sI_R)$.

Subsequent experimentation showed the need for correcting this formula. A basic correction was made by Gwynne Jones, whose revised formula, $sH_R = (D - I_R) \times (sH_R - sI_R)$, has proved to be "superior to the original one in accounting for well known phenomena."

But actual behavior does not fit such equations in every case. While they have predictive value in the generality of trials, there are occasions when sE_R will rise above or fall below expected strength. To account for this, Hull introduced the concepts of *threshold* and *oscillation*. Threshold refers to that point on the performance scale where minimum performance can be observed. Just above threshold the response is at its weakest, just below there is no response at all. However, the absence of response does not mean that learning has not occurred. In its initial stages, learning may take place without being manifested in behavior; later, behavior may not occur even though the learning has previously been confirmed by performance, presumably to be revived by an increase of D, K, or sH_R, or a decrease of I_R or sI_R sufficient to raise sE_R above threshold.

But even if we know the values of all these variables, we cannot always predict the nature of the response. Though speed and amplitude of performance will *generally* follow a curve in accordance with these values, large rises and falls will suddenly occur at random points. Hull referred to this phenomenon as oscillation. Oscillation, which is not otherwise predictable, is an acknowledgment of the limits of his system which Hull had to make to keep it in accord with experimental reality.

The principle of oscillation is useful, nevertheless, in

forecasting which of two incompatible performances competing for expression is likely to occur in a given trial. As Hill explains this:

> The oscillations of the two sE_R's are not synchronized, so that when one sE_R is momentarily high the other may be high, medium, or low. If the ranges of oscillation of the two sE_R's overlap, each response will occur on some trials. If the sE_R for one response is considerably stronger than that for the other, so that their ranges of oscillation overlap only slightly, the stronger will occur most of the time and the weaker only rarely. If the two are equally strong, so that their ranges of oscillation coincide, each will occur half of the time.

From the point of view of the organism itself, oscillation, in combination with reactive inhibition, serves the purpose of opening a new way to a goal when an old one has been blocked. As the unreinforced response entailing the old way is repeatedly tried, reactive inhibition builds up, so that the tendency to make the response lessens. At the same time, oscillation will cause alternative responses to occur, one of which may bring the goal in reach.

Another concept which we find in Hull is that of the *fractional antedating reaction*. This mouthful of polysyllables refers to a response made to a learned goal situation before the goal is reached. If a rat is repeatedly put in a maze at the end of which it will find a pellet of food, the animal will respond to the stimuli of the maze itself by salivating and licking its chops, thus antedating the reaction it will show in the presence of the goal. The reason Hull calls this reaction fractional is that a full reaction, including ingestion of the food, is not possible until the goal is actually reached. The importance of the fractional antedating reaction (r_G) is that it produces stimuli (S_G), which, because they resemble the stimuli associated with drive reduction, have a secondary reinforcing effect.

Secondary reinforcement is the tendency a neutral stimulus acquires to reinforce, when that stimulus has been paired with a reinforcer. Thus, a hungry rat which is regularly fed in a white box, if presented with a white and a black box, will consistently move toward the former, even when there is no food in it. The reinforcement for this behavior is not drive reduction, which can only be effected by primary reinforcement.

Hull also recognized *secondary drives*, which are created by pairing a neutral stimulus with a primary drive stimulus. Fear is an example of a secondary drive; it is produced by a neutral stimulus paired with the primary drive, pain. Thus cars, airplanes, white rats (as Watson showed), and nearly any other stimulus can bring on a fear reaction comparable to that of the original stimulus which conditioned it.

For all these phenomena and more, Hull developed symbols, formulas, and equations in profusion. It is impossible to do more than suggest the complexity and rigorousness of his system here. In any final evaluation, it must be said that his dream of becoming the Newton of behavioral psychology was realized only in small measure. Illness in his last years prevented Hull from doing much of the work he had planned. And enough of his formulas proved contradictory and inadequate to further laboratory testing to raise questions as to the wisdom of others going on with such a grand design, at least in the present state of experimental knowledge.

Yet this is not to suggest that his undertaking was some kind of monumental failure. His theory did inspire the work of a whole generation of students of behavior. Says Hill: "His interpretations of drive, reinforcement, extinction, and generalization are standard starting points for discussion of these topics. He has been attacked, defended, and elaborated until to many people 'learning theory' and 'Hullian theory' have become synonyms. The system of terms that he introduced has been aptly referred to by Cotton as 'the Esperanto of psychology.' "

While Hull solved the problem of Thorndike's law of effect by positing the centrality of drive, B(urrhus). F(rederic). Skinner (1904–   ) worked his way around the problem by distinguishing two types of behavior, one subject to reinforcement and one not. A 1931 doctoral graduate of Harvard who returned to teach there in 1948, Skinner recognized that certain movements were reflexive and subject to classical conditioning. He called these movements, elicited by particular stimuli, *respondent behavior*. In respondent behavior, he said, reinforcement plays no role, except as the unconditioned stimulus may reinforce the conditioned one—a position that, as the reader will recognize, he derived from Pavlov.

But respondent behavior was only one kind of behavior—and not the most significant kind, either. "Pavlov had shown the way," Skinner has written, "but I could not . . . move without a jolt from salivary reflexes to the important business of the organism in everyday life." Skinner therefore designated a second category of behavior, into which most observable actions fall, as *operant behavior*. Operant behavior differs from respondent behavior in that it operates upon the environment. Skinner does not say that operant behavior is not induced by stimuli, but—in keeping with an extreme antitheoretical stance he took from the beginning—that the stimuli are too complex and unknowable to consider in terms of predictability or control. Thus he starts with what he can observe, the behavior as *emitted* by the organism, rather than behavior presumed to be elicited by specific stimuli.

Walking, talking, working, playing, eating, fighting, jumping, drinking, sleeping, laughing are different forms of operant behavior. In contrast to respondent behavior, these depend on a large variety of circumstances and therefore such control as they can be brought under is partial and temporary.

Take walking, for example. The original thought of walking might be induced by the prior thought of a place to go. But whether the movement actually occurs will depend on the weather, social considerations, one's attachment to one's present environment, and a host of other factors. Yet it can, to a degree, be determined by rewards. If at the end of the walk, good food and pleasant company may be anticipated, the walk will more likely be undertaken than otherwise. Operant behavior followed by reinforcement will tend to recur.

But then we are back to the law of effect with its difficulties. Not quite. By eschewing theory, but not attempting to analyze the connection between reward, eliciting stimuli, and the organism's response—which he regards as a hopeless task—Skinner sidesteps any argument. This may appear questionable; however, reducing a complicated unobservable event to a simple formula that works sometimes and at other times does not is scarcely a scientific contribution. Skinner's position is that nobody knows enough about the matter to do more than venture uneducated guesses. Not only are there differences among organisms with regard to eliciting stimuli, but the reflexive repertoire of even a single organism will change as the result of learning. Control, therefore, should be the main goal of behavioral science, with prediction following once control has been achieved.

In his views on reinforcement, Skinner agrees with Hull in recognizing two kinds of reinforcers, *positive reinforcers* and *negative reinforcers*, although unlike Hull he does not relate them to drive. A positive reinforcer acts for reason of its occurrence, as when money and a meal are presented to a tramp for chopping wood. A negative reinforcer is operative upon its removal or termination. Thus, eliminating an electric shock which prevents access to a particular area of a laboratory situation will induce the animal to enter that area in the same way that food without the shock would reinforce the behavior.

Negative reinforcement obviously is related to punishment, which Skinner had considered and found wanting as a method of controlling behavior. Though negative reinforcement may suddenly stop an undesired behavior and thus appear to be dramatically successful, its effect it usually only temporary. Moreover, it tends to operate by eliciting emotional responses, such as fear and anger, which are seldom reliable adjuncts to control; they attach themselves to stimuli other than the ones the punisher hopes to render inoperative, such as the punisher himself.

The role of stimuli in operant behavior is considerably different from the simple bond which forms between stimulus and respondent in respondent behavior. If an operant is omitted when two stimuli are presented, and then the first stimulus is reinforced and the second is not, a kind of discrimination will take place. The operant will be more likely to occur with the first stimulus than with the second, the response to which will tend to be extinguished. One of Skinner's experiments in this regard involved a pigeon that was given food when it pecked a red key but not when it pecked a green key. The pigeon soon learned to peck the red key to the exclusion of the green one. But the elicitation of this response was not automatic; when satiated, the pigeon showed little inclination to peck the red key.

Experiments such as this raise questions as to when and under what conditions reinforcement is most effective. To deal with such questions, Skinner created a device that has come to be known as the *Skinner box*. Varying in size according to the organism studied, from a small box to a room, the apparatus consists of a *manipulandum* and a means for delivering a reinforcer. The manipulandum may be a lever for rats to press, a key for pigeons to peck, or a switch, handle, or plunger for humans to manipulate. The reinforcer is often food of some kind but can be anything rewarding, such as music or movies, or even escape from electric shock to the feet.

The box is operated by Skinner and his followers on the principle that reinforcers are delivered by responses to the manipulandum. Since the subject is free to emit the responses at his own rate, the later are given the name of *free operants*.

The rate at which free operants are emitted depends upon an almost unlimited number of interconnected factors, many of them unknown. Skinner and his followers have tended to concentrate on one that is independent and that can be managed, the pattern in which reinforcers follow responses, called the *schedule of reinforcement*.

Generally, two basic types of schedules have been worked out. *Continuous reinforcement* produces a reinforcer for each response to the manipulandum. In *intermittent reinforcement* reinforcement follows only some of the responses but not others.

It intermittent reinforcement is given according to the rate of response, the schedule is said to be a *ratio schedule;* if it is given following intervals of time in which responses occur, the schedule is called an *interval schedule*.

But there is more to it. Both ratio and interval schedules may be *fixed* or *variable*. In a fixed ratio schedule, the subject receives reinforcement after a set number of responses. In a fixed interval schedule, a reinforcer is delivered following response according to a pre-set timetable. If, for instance, the subject on a fixed interval schedule receives a reinforcer every two minutes, he will receive no more reinforcement if he responds once or ten times during the interval; but he will receive no reinforcement at all if, at the end of the interval, he has made no responses.

In a variable ratio schedule, the reinforcement occurs after varying numbers of operants have been emitted, so that the ratio is the average of all responses per reinforcer. Reinforcement is delivered at different set times following response on a variable interval schedule. Here, in order to get as many reinforcers as possible, the subject must respond continuously, since no pattern of reinforcement deliveries is discernible, the interval being the average of all varying periods during which reinforcement may have been available.

Numerous and detailed experiments by Skinner and his followers have shown certain general differences in response to these different kinds of schedules.

To begin with, fewer responses per reinforcer are obtained by continuous reinforcement than by any kind of intermittent reinforcement. When reinforcement is stopped altogether, resistance to extinction is greater following an intermittent than a continuous schedule. Since rapid responding on ratio schedules increases the number of reinforcers more significantly than rapid responding on interval schedules, ratio schedules, as we might expect, produce higher rates of response than interval schedules.

In both fixed ratio and fixed interval schedules, responses occur slowly following reinforcement and then increase in rate until reinforcement is given again. This phenomenon, called *scalloping,* does not occur when variable schedules are used. Skinner's explanation for this effect is that, in a fixed schedule, following reinforcement, there is less likelihood of a reinforcer being delivered again early on than later; whereas in a variable schedule the same probability doesn't exist, and there responding occurs at a more constant rate.

Under certain circumstances, the Skinner box allows us to see how what Skinner calls *superstitious behavior* comes into being. Suppose that a reinforcer is delivered every two minutes regardless of what the subject is doing. The subject may be doing nothing at all; but if he is doing something, say scratching his nose, just before delivery of the reinforcer, the response of nose scratching will be strengthened, as evidenced by an increase in its emission rate. This increase of nose scratching will make that response more likely to occur on delivery of the next reinforcer, and successive reinforcements will establish a connection between the reinforcer and the response—even though reinforcers are still being delivered without regard to any response at all.

Besides being "an impressive demonstration of the automatic operation of reinforcement," such findings lend insight to a wide variety of human behaviors which may be labeled "superstitious." On the simplest level, a boy who carries a good luck charm into an exam and receives a high mark may connect his act with the reward and take the charm with him to his next tests. If he wins a foot race while the charm is in his pocket, its general powers will be extended; and so on. Even those occasions when the "lucky charm didn't work" will not lessen the boy's faith in the connection, unless he has a severe run of non-reward which causes him to conclude that the charm has "lost its magic."

"Many of man's beliefs not only in charms and magic, but also in medicine, mechanical skills and administrative techniques," says Hill, "probably depend on such superstitious learning." Every patent remedy, no matter how worthless, has its supporters who found relief from headaches, itching, or piles which coincided with the use of the stuff. Cigarette and liquor advertising effectively, and insidiously, connects smoking and drinking with youth, wealth, and glamour in what may be considered programmed training in superstitious behavior. Indeed, much superstitious behavior in humans is probably learned from other people (as the boy may have carried his good luck charm in the first place because a friend told him of its efficacy), and then "validated" in experiences which follow Skinner's model.

One of Skinner's best-known techniques is a program of behavior modification called *shaping*. In shaping, the experimenter starts by observing the whole operant repertoire of the subject and then, by rewarding some responses and ignoring others, creates a pattern of behavior that is basically new. Thus Skinner has taught pigeons to play a form of Ping-Pong and shaped other animals' responses into patterns that are rarely seen outside of carnival sideshows. In a more serious vein, shaping has proved valuable in regularizing and bringing under control the behavior of severe schizophrenics.

In his practical concern with results and in his minimal dependence on hypothesis, Skinner is closer to Watson and Guthrie than he is to his fellow reinforcement theorists, Thorndike and Hull. But even on the practical level, the problems he sets himself are different from the ones that preoccupied the contiguity theorists. Whereas the latter sought to find the stimuli that evoked a response, Skinner typically looks for the reinforcers that sustain the response, and he has done so in hundreds of individual experiments.

It might be said that Skinner fails to tell us why one reinforcer works better than another or even why any reinforcer is reinforcing at all. But in Skinner's view, attention to such abstract questions only impedes real work. He may be right, as far as the present state of knowledge is concerned. But ultimately behavioral psychology will gain by creating a theoretical framework encompassing not only the nature of reinforcement, but everything that has been learned since Sechenev first questioned the notion of voluntary behavior.

Chapter Four

What Do We Do about
the Mind?

Tolman's Cognitive Theory

What do we do about the mind? The question has no doubt occurred to the reader at more than one point. In their concern with objectivity—dealing strictly with observable phenomena—both the contiguity and the reinforcement theorists we have looked at have seemed to speak as if the brains of animals and men were either nonexistent or no more than part of some network of experiential connections. The very attribution to them of the name "psychologist" is questionable, if we conceive psychology literally to be what it is etymologically, the study of the mind. At times, indeed, behavioral psychology appears to be an antipsychology. And this may be why some writers on the subject seem to be less comfortable with the term "behavioral psychology" than with its equivalent, "learning theory."

But even "learning theory" has something mental about it. At least in everyday usage, we think of learning as having to do with the way the brain absorbs, retains, and relates items of information and uses them for the organism's life purposes. Is such a view true, and can it be defended in experimental terms?

Edward Chase Tolman (1886–1959), who taught for

four decades at the University of California in Berkeley, answered the question affirmatively. Men and animals do not just respond to stimuli, he said, they act in accordance with knowledge and goals. His system therefore came to be called *purposive behaviorism.*

To understand the difference between Tolman and such theorists as Guthrie and Skinner let us ask the question: Given a situation, how is the organism likely to respond? Guthrie's answer would be "In the way that last changed the situation"; Skinner's would be "In the way that is most rewarding." Tolman, however, would probably say: "According to its purposes."

But how do we know what the organism's purposes really are? Many psychologies have tripped or foundered on this question. In the present state of knowledge, the best we can do is infer such purpose from the organism's actions, but such inference makes it possible for us to deal with certain kinds of behavior more adequately than the theories we have already considered allow.

Let us explore the implications of Tolman's answer a little further by posing another question. If an organism does not respond to a situation on a straight S-R basis, what happens to the stimulus and what happens to the response in such a case? Guthrie's and Skinner's answer would be that no learning takes place. Tolman's reply was to posit cognition as an *intervening variable.* The stimulus is perceived but the response does not occur because it is not in accord with the organism's purpose. This seems to take us back to Sechenev's idea of thought as "the first two thirds of the reflex"; but whereas Sechenev considered cognition as only inhibitory, Tolman regards it as a means of arriving at a successful response.

When an organism responds to a stimulus, learning occurs, but when an organism does not respond to a stimulus, a type of learning called *latent learning* may occur also. Both kinds of learning will serve the organism's future purposes, according to Tolman.

An experiment with rats illustrates this principle. The rats were placed in a maze on several nights. Each night they were taken out of the maze at different points on different occasions to insure that no path was more rewarding than any other one. Food was never put in the maze. Then the rats were starved for two days, fed in the goal box, and placed in the start box.

Half the rats took the right path to the goal box without any error, far exceeding the results of a control group which had never been in the maze. Since the right path had not previously been reinforced with food, the rat's behavior can be accounted for less easily by reinforcement principles than by latent learning.

But even had the right path been reinforced and the rats then scrambled down it to get to the food, Tolman would not have accounted for their behavior along reinforcement lines. He would still have considered their behavior purposive. In his views on reinforcement, Tolman took a position halfway between the contiguist and the reinforcement schools. He did not deny that reinforcement took place, but he did not affirm, either, that it strengthened S-R connections. He referred to rewards and punishments as "emphasizers" rather than as strengtheners or weakeners. They could lead to certain expectations rather than to others, but they did not set the limits of learning. "Tolman insisted on a distinction between learning and performance and he steadfastly refused to make a direct tie between stimulus and response."

Another experiment with rats, which Tolman conducted, provides a basis for this distinction.

The rats were placed in a complex, circuitous route at the end of which they learned to find food. Then the route was blocked and eighteen new pathways to the food were made available. Noncognitive theories lead us to expect that the rats would choose the pathways nearest to the blocked one, according to the principle of generalization. In fact, they chose the route that led most directly to the food, and this route was nowhere near the original one. Their learning had encompassed not only a pathway to food but also the location of the food in space. To designate this latter type of learning Tolman coined the term *cognitive map*. A cognitive map is not, of course, a physiological reality but a type of intervening variable.

While Watson and Guthrie recognized only one kind of learning and Skinner recognized only two kinds, Tolman distinguished six separate kinds: *cathexes, equivalence beliefs, field expectancies, cognition modes, drive discrimination,* and *motor patterns.* Of these, the first four deserve our special attention.

A cathexis is a tendency to prefer certain goals to others when experiencing a drive. Cathexes may be culturally determined—as hungry Americans will tend to seek different foods than hungry Mongolians—but any goal object that satisfies a drive will result in the formation of a cathexis. Sexual cathexes—whether heterosexual, homosexual, or bisexual—are formed under the twin influences of personal and cultural experiences, either of which may be stronger at any particular time. One of the reasons Tolman preferred to use rats in his experiments is that rats, being free of culture, behave more specifically than human beings.

Equivalence beliefs are the cognitive equivalents of conditioned reinforcers: they are beliefs that certain symbols not only stand for but are virtually identical to particular goals. Pieces of paper money, medals, and Nobel prizes are thus regarded as equivalents of wealth, recognition, and professional success. Little is known of how equivalence beliefs are acquired, but their validity seems to lie in their having wide cultural assent. The man who clips and saves magazine pictures of cakes, steaks, and turkey dinners in the belief that he is storing food is given a wide berth, but the man who clips coupons off bonds and takes them to the bank is often highly thought of.

Field expectancies are the sum of our knowledge about how the world looks, feels, smells, tastes, sounds, and how its parts relate to each other, and what they do. Cognitive maps are basically made up of items of this kind of learning. Rewards and punishments may momentarily change the way we regard our field expectancies but have no essential connection with the way they are formed.

Field cognition modes are ways of learning or tendencies to learn certain things about a situation rather than other things. Thus rats learn about the passages in a maze differently from humans, who use language to achieve such learning. But human beings of different cultures, and even individuals of the same culture, will tend to differ in their learning of the same objective situation. Varying field cognition modes may explain why several disinterested witnesses to an accident or crime will sometimes tell conflicting stories.

Of the two remaining types of learning, drive discrimination refers to learning as to which goals satisfy which drives, and motor patterns refers to muscular movements which are learned with little or no regard to cognition.

Though Tolman was almost an exact contemporary of Watson, we have treated him last because, intellectually if not chronologically, he seems to conclude the theory-building process we have been observing. From a concatenation of conditioned and unconditioned reflex movements, human and animal behavior came to be regarded by behavioral psychology as an increasingly complex affair. But "it was Tolman's contribution . . . to show that a sophisticated behaviorism can be cognizant of all the richness and variety of psychological events, and need not be constrained by an effort to build an engineer's model of the learning machine."

Curiously, Tolman has had few direct followers. More recent attempts to explain cognitive phenomena in behavioral terms have come from reinforcement theorists seeking to broaden their position. The antimental inheritance of Watson has proved to be as much a burden as a blessing to behavioral psychology. But in the day when a comprehensive and definitive theory of learning can be built, that theory will surely have the precision that Hull strove for, combined with the insight that makes Tolman stand apart.

Part Three:

HUMAN BEHAVIOR
MODIFICATION

A habit is a consistent way of responding to defined stimulus conditions. Ordinarily a habit declines—undergoes extinction—when its consequences become unadaptive . . . . Neurotic habits are distinguished by their resistance to extinction in the face of their unadaptiveness. Behavior therapy, as far as neurotic habits are concerned, is mainly the application of experimentally established principles of learning to overcome these habits, but sometimes the conditioning of positive new habits is a major goal. In order to change a habit it is always necessary to involve the individual responses that constitute it. Change depends on eliciting behavior that can compete with these individual responses.

JOSEPH WOLPE (1969)

Chapter Five

Behavior Therapy

General Principles

If all behavior follows the laws of learning, abnormal behavior should also be learned behavior, and such is the case in behavioral psychology. There is nothing "sick" about abnormal behavior; it is learned in the same way as so-called normal behavior; it differs from the latter only in that it is unadaptive. This is a basic principle of behavior therapy.

The principal may be illustrated by recalling Watson's experiment with Albert B. Little Albert was conditioned to fear a white rat by a gong being struck whenever the harmless small creature was introduced. Now, it is unadaptive to be afraid of white rats. In childhood, they are given one as pets or one's friends have them as pets; in adulthood, particularly if one is interested in the biological or behavioral sciences, contact with them may be useful or necessary. In both cases, one's phobia seems queer to one's associates and queer and disturbing to one's self, because it is neither based on any danger nor universally shared. Most people's conditioning to white rats is undergone with pleasurable stimuli—a feeling of possession and control, the sensation of soft fur, tickling, and perhaps the laughter of others.

But suppose the animal Watson introduced when he struck the gong had been a rattlesnake. Even if Albert's resultant fear had generalized to other kinds of snakes —harmless as well as dangerous ones—the learning would have been adaptive. Herpetophiles to the contrary, it is usually more important to turn away from an unknown snake than to pause to discriminate among species. And because some degree of fear of snakes is universal in our culture, Albert would not have had to feel queer or different about his phobia.

But the matter goes further. Fear and anxiety have acquired a bad name in our time, largely from the psychodynamic psychologists, who identify it with neurosis, but if we compare a fear of snakes with a fear of harmless or useful animals, we see that anxiety is merely neutral and functional, a "mediating drive" as H. J. Eysenck calls it, and that its adaptiveness or maladaptiveness depends on what is feared and the consequences of the fear. A fear of snakes is a fear that will be shared, approved, commended—in short, reinforced. A fear of white rats will be laughed at and scorned—in short, punished. It will give rise to a welter of unpleasant emotions, including a heightened anxiety which arises from the undesired and "irrational" nature of the fear itself. Learning theory has a scant regard for punishment as a means of changing behavior; so the fear will persist in the face of the most persistent mockery.

Watson imagined little Albert's fear persisting into his adulthood. Perhaps. But if the fear was easily induced by conditioning, it may also have been easily extinguished by conditioning.

It will be recalled that Pavlov observed individual differences in conditionability among his dogs. Behavior therapists, not surprisingly, recognize the same to be the case with humans. Some people condition easily and maintain their conditioned responses over many trials; other people require numerous pairings of the unconditioned and conditioned stimuli to learn a response and then "lose" the response after a few trials. "Watson was lucky in his choice of subject; others have banged away with hammers on metal bars in an attempt to condition infants, but not always with the same success." Thus Watson might have imagined Albert, still a boy, reconditioned to white rats in the presence of happy, playful companions, in a real-life reenactment of Mary Cover Jones's experiment with little Peter.*

The role of individual susceptibility in conditioning has, for obvious reasons, been of greater concern to behavior therapists than to learning theorists, who are interested chiefly in discovering basic laws. The latter may tell us that an intense stimulus or a strong reinforcement is more likely to evoke a response than a weak one, and this is valuable information to have in treating patients with behavior problems. But the ultimate effectiveness of therapy will depend not only on technique but on the character of the patient himself, specifically on the speed and firmness with which he is able to develop conditioned responses or to show modification of operant behavior.

High conditionability has been shown to be a quality of the *introvert* type of person—the type that tends to be thoughtful, peaceable, quiet, considerate of others. A high degree of autonomic reactivity is characteristic of the person with a tendency to *neuroticism*. Where introversion and neuroticism occur together, behavior therapists expect to find an individual who suffers from anxieties, compulsions, obsessions, conditioned fears, and reactive depressions. Such an individual is said to be *dysthymic*.

The individual who is unable to form quick and strong conditioned responses is less likely to suffer from fears and anxieties, but he is also less likely to form conditioned responses which make for his thorough socialization. He is the *extravert*—voluble, outgoing, persistent, with little regard for others. When this type of individual has a high degree of autonomic reactivity, he is likely to exhibit the neurotic traits of the *psychopath* or *hysteric*: aggressiveness, violence, and criminal behavior. He is, in a way, the neurotic introvert turned inside out; what the latter suffers himself, the neurotic extravert inflicts on others. Between these two extremes fall all

* Described in Chapter One.

other classes of neurotic people—including, of course, the so-called normal ones, somewhere in the middle. As Aubrey Yates has pointed out, the exhibit of a neurotic symptom is not in itself proof of neuroticism; such a symptom, like Albert's fear, may be conditioned in the most normal person. Yates therefore distinguishes between monosymptomatic and polysymptomatic abnormalities, the latter being characteristic of neurotics.

The classification of their patients into these types bears no relation to the purposes with which such classification—usually into many more types—is undertaken by psychodynamic therapists. The latter's categories aim toward identifying the dynamic by which the symptoms are produced, so that the underlying elements of the neurosis can be identified and released to consciousness. Behavior therapists are interested primarily in conditionability. Regardless of what repressed material may or may not lie buried, it is obviously important to know whether a patient will condition easily or with difficulty in prescribing a course of treatment for him. In this connection, Eysenck's remarks about the treatment of psychopaths are illuminating.

I have shown how psychopathic reactions originate because of the inability of the psychopath, due to his low level of conditionability, to acquire the proper socialized responses. But this failure is not absolute; he conditions much less quickly and strongly than others, but he does condition. Thus, where the normal person may need 50 pairings of the conditioned and the unconditioned stimulus and where the dysthymic may need 10, the psychopath may require 100. But presumably in due course the 100 pairings will be forthcoming, although probably much later in life than the 10 of the dysthymic, or the 50 of the normal person, and then he will finally achieve a reasonable level of socialization. If this chain of reasoning is correct, it would lead us to expect that the diagnosis "psychopath" would by and large be confined to relatively young people, say under thirty years of age; after thirty the course of life should have brought forth the required 100 pairings and thus produced the needed amount of socialization. As far as I can ascertain, clinical psychiatric opinion is in agreement with this position.

By comparison, treatment of a dysthymic, while easier from the standpoint of conditioning individual symptoms, may be just as laborious as treatment of a psychopath because of the multiplicity of symptoms the dysthymic presents. And his tendency to evidence new symptoms *because* of his high conditionability may necessitate the dysthymic's return to therapy long after the original symptoms have been extinguished.

But this possibility in no way affirms the psychodynamic argument that the treatment of behavior problems is futile because it fails to deal with the underlying neurosis which causes them to appear. According to this argument, a child cured of bed wetting by conditioning will then exhibit a stammer or some other behavioral abnormality.

Behavioral practice, however, shows such symptom substitution to be the exception rather than the rule. Bed wetting, once cured by conditioning therapy, stays cured in most cases. If the condition returns, as we might expect in terms of learning theory, it yields rapidly to repeated treatment. Nor do other undesirable behaviors occur that may not be traceable to altogether different conditioning factors.

According to psychodynamic theory, the removal of a symptom should result in a heightening of anxiety. Behavior therapists like Cyril M. Franks have observed quite the opposite.

. . . in many instances, far from emotional training causing, say bed wetting, it is the bed wetting that brings about the emotional disturbance. So perhaps, rather than criticizing improvement as being merely symptomatic, one might better regard the disappearance or amelioration of the symptom as in itself one of the major criteria of improvement. Such available evidence as there is tends to suggest not only that symptoms fail to recrudesce but that, on the contrary, the removal of one symptom tends also to facilitate the removal of others by decreasing the patient's over-all anxiety level, improving his personal feelings of well-being, and thus helping him develop in the area of interpersonal relationships.

Curiously enough, in one of the few regions where Freudian theory lends itself to making testable predictions it fails to obtain support!*

If dysthymics and psychopaths are distinguishable by their relative conditionability or unconditionability, the difference should be quantifiable in these terms. This is suggested by Eysenck in a general way. "On the one hand we have *surplus conditioned reactions,*" that is, a great number of conditioned responses acquired in the course of living, including ones which are "unadaptive even though originally they may have been well suited to circumstances. On the other hand we have *deficient conditioned reactions,* that is, reactions normally acquired by most individuals in society which are adaptive, but which because of defective conditioning powers have not been acquired by a particular person."

Eysenck, however, cautions that conditionability is only a *potential* and that the amount of social conditioning a person has acquired depends on an interplay with environmental factors. Obviously, an individual who cannot form conditioned responses at all—an extreme psychopath—will never be socialized. But by the same token, an individual of the most puissant conditionability will not be socialized, either, if he grows up on a desert island, or he will be socialized unadaptively for one culture if he grows up in another which is vastly different.

The implications of this view are exciting, not only from a therapeutic standpoint, but also in terms of social analysis and planning. It may be possible, for instance, to show that poverty and crime are not only connected by material want but by lack of suitable conditioning. Poor people cannot respond successfully to important social cues they may not even be aware of and thus stand at a disadvantage to others who have learned the proper responses to these cues in the course of growing up. In as

* The behaviorist counterattack on the Freudians has grown stronger with the increasing success of behavior therapy, Joseph Wolpe, for instance calling for an end to the study of psychoanalysis in the training of psychotherapists.

basic a matter as the job interview, poor people will, in their dress, speech, and manner, exhibit conditioning that seems inappropriate to the prospective employer, and this results in their not getting the job. Such experiences, multiplied many times, eventually cause poor people to feel like outsiders. From outsider to outlaw is a small step, especially when need and want are present as catalysts for the transformation.

In recent years, the literature of behavior therapy has shown an increasing number of cases of the application of learning theory to the treatment of psychotics. Two facts have emerged from various experiments conducted with psychotic patients, chiefly in the last decade and a half; psychotics are conditionable and they seem particularly responsive to operant techniques.

In one case, psychotic speech was reduced in thirteen weeks from 90 to 50 percent of the patient's verbalization by withdrawal of attention to the psychotic speech. In another, delusional speech in a sixty-year-old man was reduced from forty-three minutes to 15 minutes per forty-five-minute session by the therapist ignoring the delusional speech and reinforcing rational speech with nods and smiles. A follow-up study two years later found the patient capable of producing rational speech 93 percent of the time with minimal reinforcement and 100 percent of the time with maximal reinforcement. In still another case, two catatonic males who had not emitted verbal responses in over fourteen years were conditioned to make meaningful sounds with rewards of candy.

The subject of speech leads us naturally to language. The arrangement of human sounds into meaningful patterns is the one area of behavior about which behavior therapists have learned less from learning theory than from general semantics.*

If they considered language at all, most learning

* In recent years learning theorists have begun to investigate the function of language in human behavior. Notable in this respect is the work of Charles Osgood and his associates at the University of Illinois.

theorists, as we have seen, set it down as a type of complex learning or as operant behavior, in either case no different, say, from walking. In behavior therapy, language has come to occupy a quite central position. Not only is it the means by which the patient reports his symptoms—and by which the therapist sets down his history—it also functions as an instrument of treatment. Therapeutic conditioning is carried out not only with objects like bells and shocks and morsels of food but also with words.

The resistance of the early learning theorists to language was based, it will be recalled, on a desire to create a purely objective science. When Thorndike and Watson began their studies, psychology was suffused with a variety of specious theories which nobody had bothered to prove in the laboratory. Phrenology, the pseudo-science by which cranial bumps were "read" to determine personality, was still very respectable. (The "classic" 1911 edition of the *Encyclopedia Britannica* devotes seven tightly printed, sober pages to its theory and history.) This kind of nonsense had been produced with words—which were unceasingly capable of producing more nonsense.

A second source of resistance to language was its invisibility. Facts and feelings could be reported in words but they couldn't be seen, measured, or verified. Therefore, even if they existed, they had no importance unless they registered as items of behavior.

Finally, there was the force of circumstance. Most early behavioral experiments were done with rats, cats, and dogs, and to this day behavioral psychologists use animals extensively. Even when human subjects are employed, they are often given problems of the kind that animals are put to solve, to wit, nonverbal ones.

Now, animals don't have language—at least of a kind that most behavioral psychologists can understand. Human beings do. And for them language functions not only as a medium of foolishness and error but importantly as a second signaling system with which they respond to each other and to their environment. This fact does not in any way invalidate any of learning theory. Conceivably, learning theory might not have developed to the point it has, if undue regard had been paid to language. And another defense must be made: the behavioral experimenters were primarily interested in discovering the principles that govern behavior as such, without regard to the individual or species.

But the difference between theory and therapy in this matter need not be exaggerated. In a real sense, what the behavior therapist has learned about language tends only to confirm and extend what learning theory has said about behavior in general. Words function in the same manner as operants and conditioned stimuli. They produce consequences and elicit responses. They induce, shape, modify, and control behavior.

The ability of the demagogue to move masses of men with language to cheer, march, wreck, and even kill is a theme that runs through all of history and literature. The behavior of a mob is terrible and irrational, but in its own way adheres to the laws of learning. The demagogue knows that people respond to certain words and phrases with conditioned aversion—communist, capitalist, colonialist, Jew, Catholic, Wall Street, foreigner— according to the time and culture. He uses such words to build up extremes of hostile emotion in his listeners, reinforcing their responses with his own sneers and snarls. When this process has reached its culmination, he has only to suggest a course of action—"Let's burn down the town"—and his listeners may do just that.

Not only do wicked people use words to elicit destructive behavior, but good or well-meaning people use them to promote behavior that is desirable. Psychotherapists condition their patients to engage in certain kinds of actions and to desist from other kinds by labeling the former "mature" and the latter "immature." The words are translated by the patient to mean, respectively, "I approve" and "I disapprove." Clergymen speak of peace, heaven, and morality to encourage kindly behavior; that their efforts are not always successful suggests that the efficacy of their verbal equipment to induce the intended conditioned responses may be waning. When the late President Kennedy said, "Ask not what your country can do for you, ask what you can do for your country," part of a generation of young people went to the four corners of the world to serve in the Peace Corps. "Serve" and "country" were words that could move people, at least here and then.

How such words achieve the status of behavioral stimuli depends on the circumstances in which they are learned; that is, how we are conditioned to them. If we grow up in a culture where our parents, teachers, and peers speak words like "Jew" and "black" disparagingly, our behavior toward individuals who bear these labels will be affected by such conditioning. Years ago, Carey McWilliams observed that anti-Semitism was likely to be stronger in places where there were few or no Jews than where Jews were numerous. Anti-black attitudes, also, are likely to be stronger in inverse proportion to the number of blacks whom one has known. In both cases, the power of verbal conditioning must be acknowledged. Indeed, even one's responses to white rats and snakes are more likely to be shaped by verbal stimuli than by psychologists striking gongs.

What has been said about words applies to other kinds of symbols—flags, crucifixes, medals, red and green lights, uniforms: all of these are capable of influencing or determining behavior. And not only overt behavior but internal physiological processes as well.

The late Dr. Gregory Razran illustrated the principles of Pavlovian psychology by teaching his students to salivate in response to the words "urn" and "style." With some of his subjects he was able to demonstrate the process of generalization by inducing salivation with the synonyms "vase" and "fashion."

Russian psychophysiologists have achieved dilation and contraction of the stomach muscles by symbolic conditioning. Informed that their stomachs were being warmed, a group of subjects showed stomach muscle dilations, though nothing was actually changing the temperature of their stomachs; told that their stomachs were being cooled, they responded with a tightening of the same muscles. Similar experiments have been carried on by the Russians using red and blue lights to produce opposite internal reactions. In one instance, the lights were flashed in random sequences. The subjects became ill, conplained of headaches, sensory distortions, and nausea, and actually vomited. This suggests to behavior therapists a cause of psychosomatic disorders in which mutually incompatible learned conditioned responses are involved.

We have been looking at language as a dimension of human behavioral processes, and it is. In most cases the words that people speak or hear are consonant with other dimensions of their experience or behavior, but in other cases they are not. The child who is told by his parents "I love you, Johnny," and then is regularly beaten, the student who is taught by his teachers that he lives in the best of countries and then observes a politics rife with corruption, will in varying degrees learn to make distinctions between words and the things they stand for. To a certain extent, this is normal; words do not always mean what they are supposed to. The value of living itself is in going beyond the limits of language —traveling the terrain of reality rather than what is printed on maps, whether the "maps" be made of words or lines drawn on a chart. But there are people so conditioned by their life experience that language per se is suspect.

"To such persons," as Andrew Salter says, "a word becomes the thing-that-you-do-the-opposite-of. . . . The environment is a chronic enemy. Words-from-others are never words-for-me." Such persons have to have their responses to words reconditioned before language can be used in their therapy.

"What I do," Salter relates,

> . . . is to try to recondition their verbal systems all at once. "Pavlov," I explain, "spoke of a reflex of freedom and a reflex of slavery. Now," I continue, "you call what you are doing freedom. I doubt that it is true freedom,

but let it pass. However, what I want to do with you is to restore your reflex of slavery, to a point. Yes, reflex of slavery. I want to make you a slave again."

This horrifies them, of course. I then explain their self-defeating negativistic conditioning . . . and as I explain how to become a slave—how to let the environment dominate, how to surrender— . . . with concrete illustrations from their personal life, more often than not we make substantial progress in a half-dozen sessions, after the first preliminary ones.

A half-dozen sessions! The reader who may be conditioned to the talk therapies deriving from psychodynamic psychology (which have no time limits) must respond with some surprise. Behavior therapy is characteristically a no-nonsense, short-term affair.

There is no "transference" (patient's deep feeling for the therapist) or "countertransference" (therapist's corresponding feeling for the patient) required, and if one occurs, it is not encouraged. The therapist–patient relationship is much like that between any professional and a layman who seeks his services, whether the professional be a doctor, lawyer, or stockbroker. And just as a doctor, lawyer, or stockbroker, after listening to his client's problems and goals, draws up a program of action to be followed, so does the behavior therapist.

He does not sit back and ask the patient to talk on for hours, hoping that at the end of 900 such hours (the average course of psychoanalysis) a resolution of the problems will somehow emerge. He gets down to work as quickly as possible, confident of the techniques at his disposal. The words he elicits from the patient are not accounts of dreams and fantasies but have to do specifically with the unadaptive behavior to be attacked: its history, the conditions under which it appears, and the factors that may be reinforcing it. When he has this information, the behavior therapist then takes over. He is unequivocally directive. "This is what we're going to do," he says and then proceeds to do it. If one approach doesn't work, he tries another. He never blames the patient when progress is not made.

Because of its coolness and efficiency, behavior therapy has been charged with being "a psychotherapy without soul." The charge is superficially true; behavior therapy has no more "soul" than heart surgery or dentistry, yet it has no less interest in promoting the well-being of the patient than other therapies. The ultimate question is whether psychotherapy has to be a long, deep, agonized confrontation between therapist and patient or whether it should move as rapidly as possible to provide relief and restore the patient to normal functioning. Behavior therapy chooses the latter course.

Its statistics are impressive. One behavior therapist (Lazarus) reports a mean of 9.5 sessions in eighteen cases in which children were cured of phobias. Follow-ups of from six months to two years showed no relapses. Two physicians (Burnett and Ryan) who treated 100 neurotic patients on learning theory principles for an average course of five weeks were able to follow up a fourth of these patients for a year or more. They reported that 60 percent were still either apparently cured or much improved and 32 percent were moderately improved. Joseph Wolpe has reported recoveries of 90 percent among 210 neurotics whom he treated on such short-term bases. By comparison, the *best* recovery figures for psychoanalysis—which do not include patients who, for whatever reasons, fail to complete their analyses—fall into the low sixtieth percentile.

In the next chapter we shall look at some of the techniques that behavior therapists use to eliminate abnormal behavior, along with some actual cases. But a few words still need to be said in this general discussion of the relationship between learning theory and behavior therapy. We have used the term "learning theory" as if it stood for a unified body of knowledge on which everybody agreed. We know that this is far from being the case. Contiguity theorists argue with reinforcement theorists about the necessity and utility of reinforcement, and cognition theorists often disagree with both. Yet such disputes take on an air of the academic in therapeutic practice. Behavior therapists, we may say, are conditioned by their role to be more pragmatic and eclectic. They deal with people who are unhappy with the ways they behave and who look for changes rather than hypotheses. The individual therapist may start out from a particular theoretical position, but his main questions, when he is faced by a patient in need, have to do with what will work—what will most effectively produce extinction of undesirable behavior and introduce desirable behavior in its place. And he is more likely to seek answers in past therapeutic experiences than in theoretical models.

Moreover, the analysis of any particular case in terms of its underlying theory is usually susceptible to more than one, or to several interpretations.

A single example will illustrate this point. In 1960, D. Walton of Warrington, England, reported his treatment of a twenty-year-old woman with neuro-dermatitis. The condition, which was of two years standing, was seated on the nape of the patient's neck. The young woman scratched the irritation persistently, often bringing blood.

She had been treated by two general practitioners and a skin specialist, who had prescribed pills, ointments, lotions, and X-ray therapy without result. Finally, she was referred to Walton, a clinical psychologist, because there seemed to be a relation between the continuance of the illness and her family's attention to it.

Besides the young woman herself, the family consisted of a father, a mother, and an older brother. The family was not well-to-do, but the father was ambitious for his children, particularly the son, whom he preferred to the daughter. Every Sunday the father and son would go out for a walk and return late in the afternoon, often causing the midday meal to be spoiled by their tarrying. When the son went off to college, much of the family income was set aside for his fees, clothes, and books. In contrast, his sister, still in grammar school, was given barely enough for clothes and other needs, and the father showed more interest in her brother's progress than in hers.

With the onset of her dermatitis, the situation changed. Not only did the girl receive more attention than she had ever received before from her family, she was getting attention from professionals, as well. In addition, she had become engaged, and her fiancé was also concerned about her condition. On arriving at the young woman's home, he would rub ointment into her neck.

Walton hypothesized that although "the skin condition may well have originated because of physical conditions . . . the rewards initially associated with the continuance of the neuro-dermatitis had reinforced the scratching until it had become a powerful compulsive habit and it was this which had directly perpetuated the skin condition."

After this, treatment and cure were swift. To effect extinction of the habit, Walton instructed the "members of [the young woman's] family . . . not to discuss her skin condition with her, in fact to observe, as far as possible, a complete silence on the subject. The application of ointment by the fiancé was also to stop."

Following these measures, the frequency of the scratching progressively decreased until it stopped altogether after two months. Correspondingly, the dermatitis gradually lessened until it was gone in three months. A follow-up four years later found the young woman happily married for three years, successfully employed as a solicitor, and with "no evidence of the neuro-dermatitis [or of any other skin condition] over this period."

According to what laws of learning had this happy outcome been achieved? A Guthrian psychologist might argue that the "combination of stimuli" (the family's and the boyfriend's attentions) that had "accompanied the movement" (scratching) had, by the therapist's directions, been removed, thus lessening the tendency of the movement to recur. A Skinnerian might analyze Walton's success in terms of the elimination of the consequences that reinforced the patient's operant behavior. And both would be right, theoretically. Walton himself analyzed the therapy after the Hullian model, according to which resistance to a response builds up with nonreinforcement until the response is extinguished. And, of course, *he* was right.

Chapter Six

The Therapist's

Techniques

Reciprocal Inhibition, Assertive Training, Negative Practice, et al.

In 1947–1948 Joseph Wolpe of the University of Witwaterstrand in South Africa* conducted a series of experiments with cats. Out of these experiments came a basic model for much of the behavioral therapeutic practice carried on to this day.

Wolpe placed his cats in an experimental cage, and "after presenting an auditory stimulus, [subjected] them to a small number of high-voltage, low-amperage shocks from an induction coil. . . . The animals all reacted violently to the shocks, showing various combinations of rushing to and fro; clawing at the roof, floor and sides of the cage; crouching, trembling, howling and spitting. . . ." When the animals were removed from the cage, the symptoms lessened. But each time they were returned to the

---

* The pioneers of modern behavior therapy—such as Wolpe, Eysenck, Lazarus, Rachman, Liversedge, Sylvester, Meyer, Raymond, and Yates—have by and large come from outside the United States. At least till very recently, what passed for behavior therapy in this country was really a hybrid of behavioral and psychodynamic psychology, such as we find espoused in Dollard and Miller's *Personality and Psychotherapy*. There is a curious irony in the fact that foreign therapists were the first to apply learning principles discovered in America, while their American counterparts largely subordinated these principles to a psychodynamic theory which originated in Europe.

cage they exhibited the same frantic behavior again. Confinement in the cage for several hours at a time brought no diminution in the reactions, nor did months of absence from its environs.

It was clear to Wolpe that the animals' anxiety responses were different from other kinds of ineffectual responses, which could be extinguished by fatigue and the removal of reinforcement; the cats' neurotic behavior "would have to be regarded as permanent and irreversible," Wolpe decided.

However, he considered that if another response, incompatible with that behavior, could be induced, it might in time be made to supersede the latter. Eating was an obvious such alternative response. The problem was that the animals, even if starved for as long as seventy-two hours, would not so much as touch food dropped in front of them while they were in the experimental cage.

But they did eat in their living cages, where they were fed by hand. The human hand was thus introduced as a feeding stimulus in the experimental cage. While *none* of the cats would eat in the experimental cage before, *some* would take food there from a hand-held rod. And these cats subsequently ate food offered in this manner with decreasing hesitation.

Of the cats which still would not eat, Wolpe observed that all reacted with anxiety not only to the experimental cage but also to the laboratory in which it was contained, as well as to a series of other rooms which bore various features of resemblence to the laboratory. But a place could be found where each of these remaining cats could initially be induced to eat, in a room that was nearly like the laboratory or less so. Presumably, this place did not evoke anxiety to the extent that it inhibited the eating response.

Gradually, a cat who would feed in a room appreciably different in appearance from the laboratory could be induced to eat in a room more closely resembling it, and then in a room still more similar to the laboratory, and so on. After some days of such progress, the cat could be made to feed in the laboratory itself and, finally, even in the experimental cage, without exhibiting any signs of anxiety.

However, the anxiety responses could be evoked again by presenting the auditory stimulus (CS) which had preceded the shocks (US). Wolpe was able to extinguish these responses to the sound in a manner similar to that which had rendered the visual stimuli noneffective.

While feeding the animals, he produced the auditory stimulus at a sufficient distance from them so that the anxiety it evoked was not great enough to interfere with the eating response. Gradually, the stimulus could be brought closer until—after some days—the animals would eat in its presence at the original loudness, without manifesting anxiety. As might be expected, the auditory stimulus became linked with the feeding stimulus; but extinction of the animals' response to it by repeated nonreinforcement did not lead to a return of the anxiety.

In broad outline, Wolpe's experiments illustrate the principal of *reciprocal inhibition*, which may be stated as follows. If a normal response incompatible with an unadaptive one is induced in the presence of the stimuli which evoke the latter, the bond between those stimuli and the unadaptive response will weaken. But the experiments also present paradigms of the principles of *systematic desensitization* and *extinction* as well. All of these terms are used to describe particular behavioral therapy procedures. In practice, however, as in the experiments, they rarely occur in a pure or isolated form. Thus, reciprocal inhibition—sometimes also called *counter-conditioning*—frequently requires the patient's systematic desensitization to the stimulus which evokes his maladaptive behavior in order for a new response to the counter-stimulus to occur—as Wolpe's cats were systematically desensitized to the stimuli of the cage and the sound before they would eat. Similarly, the extinction of a neurotic response is often an affair of systematic desensitization to the stimulus which elicits it. And some therapists argue that extinction of a neurotic response does not occur without another response—perhaps unperceived—taking its place; in other words, that extinction in essence involves reciprocal inhibition. For all these reasons the three terms—extinction, reciprocal inhibition, and systematic desensitization—are sometimes used interchangeably, though they define different phenomena or different aspects of the same process.

CASE HISTORY (Wolpe). A twenty-three-year-old man showing symptoms of extreme anxiety told the following story. A tram motorman, he had been driving slowly when a woman walked into his vehicle. She was knocked unconscious and there was blood on her head. Although a doctor told him that the injury wasn't serious, in the eight hours since the accident he had become increasingly shaky and developed acute abdominal pain.

The patient's history was taken over a course of five interviews, during which he revealed a fear of human blood, which he said he had had ever since his father had died in an accident when the young man was thirteen. Now even a tiny drop of blood from a shaving cut made him feel uneasy. That human blood was the anxiety-inducing stimulus was confirmed by two other statements: the young man had recovered from other accidents in which no human injury had been involved, and he was quite indifferent to the sight of animal blood: he had seen oxen slaughtered and had himself slit the throats of fowl without turning a hair.

At the fifth interview, reporting that he was feeling well again, the young man was told to drive the tram a short distance. This he did afterward without ill effect.

From the sixth interview onward, the patient, while in a state of hypnotic relaxation, was asked to imagine various situations involving blood. These were arranged in an ascending order of disturbing effect—much like the order of the rooms in which the anxiety of the cats was progressively overcome. Least disturbing was a slightly blood-tinged bandage in a basket; next was a droplet of blood on the patient's face. As he learned to respond without anxiety to each image, a new, more bloody one would be presented in its place. Thus was the young man offered two or three images per session, until he "could visualize a casualty ward full of carnage and not be disturbed by it."

In this case we have an example of extinction of a neurotic response produced by systematic desensitization: that is, the response was made to disappear by the patient gradually being inured to the stimulus that elicited it. But how do we know that the techniques, involving, of course, verbal suggestion, achieved a transfer in real life? Because as it happens, two days after the final interview, the patient witnessed an accident in which a man was knocked down by a motorcycle and bled profusely. Not only was the patient unaffected by the blood, but he helped carry the victim into the ambulance. But then wasn't something more than mere extinction involved? Seemingly, a new, reciprocal response to the sight of human blood had at that moment taken the place of the old one. Indeed, it might be said that the proof of extinction of the original phobia was precisely the patient's ability to evidence another response to the same stimulus in its place.

CASE HISTORY (Lazarus). Carol M., age nine and a half, was brought to therapy with a variety of behavioral disorders, including fear of the dark and enuresis. At school she regularly developed abdominal pains so severe that she would have to be sent home from class.

The child's history indicated that she had been healthy and well adjusted until two months after her ninth birthday, when she was exposed to three traumatic events within a few weeks. "A school friend had fallen into a pond and drowned; her next door playmate had contracted meningitis and died; she had witnessed a motor car accident in which a man was killed." About this time also, Carol's mother had read an article which said that nine-year-olds should not be given overt demonstrations of affection, lest these hinder the development of "personality and maturity." Carol's mother had behaved accordingly, shielding the child from such emotional displays. The therapist condemned the article, told Carol's mother that overt demonstrations of affection were precisely what the child required, and gave her instructions in this regard.

Then the family went away on vacation for three weeks. Shortly after their return, Carol's mother telephoned the therapist. During the vacation, she said Carol had behaved quite normally, but since coming home she had wet her bed every night and become hysterical on being taken to school.

When Carol resumed therapy it was obvious that her condition had grown worse. She was extremely tense and clung to her mother, insisting that her mother be present during all interviews.

The interviews revealed—and projective testing confirmed—that Carol's fear had nothing to do with going to sleep or to school, but with the possibility that when she awoke from sleep or returned from school she would find her mother dead. Psychoanalysts might interpret her behavior in terms of the so-called death wish; however, no inferred constructs were needed to trace the origins of Carol's condition, and the therapist sought none. He "simply regarded the child's neurotic reactions as having been precipitated by her sudden and harsh exposure to the traumatic realities of death. Since Carol's premature awareness of the finality of death had coincided with her mother's misinformed attitude toward display of love and affection, the child's consequent feelings of rejection finally culminated in a genuine fear of permanent maternal deprivation (i.e., death). Thus even a brief period of separation from her mother aggravated Carol's anxieties."

In accordance with this analysis, a hierarchy of anxiety-producing items was constructed, ranging from separation from the mother for five minutes to separation from the mother for a whole week. While fully relaxed, Carol was presented with the least noxious situation ("Imagine that you are not going to see your mother for five minutes"). When she was able to entertain this idea without ill effect, the next least noxious situation was offered up ("Imagine that you are not going to see your mother for fifteen minutes"); and so on through a progression of eight such situations to the last.

The course of therapy required five sessions over a period of ten days. The day after the final session Carol went cheerfully to school. The symptoms that had revealed themselves in the classroom did not recur, and the nighttime fears and enuresis also immediately vanished. A follow-up fifteen months later revealed that, except for a very occasional bed-wetting incident, Carol's behavior had become completely satisfactory.

Here again systematic desensitization leads to the extinction of maladaptive behavior which leads to the acquisition of new behavior that had been inhibited by the old.

Further similarities in the treatment of the cases of Carol and the motorman deserve to be noted. In both, the therapist taking the patient's history was able to pinpoint the probable origin of the maladaptive behavior. But this was the origin only insofar as the patient knew; possibly, early repressed or forgotten experiences—involving human blood for the motorman and her mother's death for Carol—were operative in their respective cases. If so, the difference is unimportant insofar as modern behavior therapy is concerned. In fact, had both patients been mutes afflicted with loss of memory, the therapist could have treated them both solely in terms of their responses. As we shall see later, operant therapy starts with the behavior to be extinguished and pays little or no attention to what preceded it. With psychotics this is often all the therapist can do. However, the patient's history is useful in revealing those elements in his life that reinforce the behavior, like Carol's mother's denial of shows of affection. As in the case of the young woman with neuro-dermatitis, which we considered in the last chapter, it is sometimes possible to extinguish unadaptive behavior simply by eliminating the factors that reward it.

In both the motorman's and Carol's cases, the maladaptive behavior was related to a single fear, and the hierarchies they were asked to experience comprised increasingly disturbing situations involving that one fear. But what of the dysthymic whose fears fall in a considerable variety of areas? Wolpe gives us a list produced by an actual patient of his as she composed it.

1. high altitudes
2. elevators
3. crowded places
4. church
5. darkness—movies, etc.
6. being alone
7. marital relations (pregnancy)
8. walking any distance
9. death
10. accidents
11. fire
12. fainting
13. falling back
14. injections
15. medications
16. fear of the unknown
17. losing one's mind
18. locked doors
19. amusement park rides
20. steep stairways

In dealing with such a mixed list, the therapist first categorizes the items as they relate to specific problems. For instance, from the list above, Wolpe identified four neurotic types of fears and six others, such as fears of death, accidents, and fires, which he labeled as "basically objective." One of the neurotic categories was fear of illness and its associations. This included items 12, 13, 14, and 15. In themselves, these did not comprise a hierarchy that could be used in systematic desensitization. Consequently, the patient was questioned further, and a list of eleven items, starting with "sight of bandages" at the weakest level, and extending to "feeling of being about to lose consciousness" at the most noxious, was produced. Where a bundle of fears is presented by the patient, each fear is worked on in turn, with its separate specific list.

It will be recalled that in the treatment of both Carol and the tram driver, the patient was put in a state of deep relaxation, the tram driver by hypnosis (drugs are also used). Relaxation is an important component of systematic desensitization, and training in deep relaxation, taking up as many as the first six or more interviews, often accompanies the construction of hierarchies. Since relaxation is the obverse of anxiety, which sustains the unadaptive behavior, its usefulness can readily be understood. Relaxation is particularly efficacious where anxiety is the main inhibitory factor to behavior which the patient desires, as in the following case of impotence.

CASE HISTORY (Wolpe). Mr. S., a forty-year-old accountant, had first gone to a psychoanalyst to remedy his impotence. When told that the treatment might take two years, he switched to a behavior therapist because, he said, the woman he loved could not be kept waiting so long.

Mr. S.'s history was taken over the course of nine interviews. It revealed that during puberty he had masturbated a good deal and been told that masturbation could lead to impotence. When he was twenty-two, he had a girl friend with whom he petted to the point of mutual orgasm. Noticing that his ejaculations were occurring with increasing swiftness, he became concerned, especially after an uncle told him that this was "a partial impotence." When he finally persuaded the girl friend to have coitus with him, he ejaculated prematurely. Soon after, she left him.

After another sexual relationship in which prematurity continued, Mr. S. married at twenty-nine. The union, which lasted nine years, was stormy in the extreme, and invariably was marked by emission before penetration in the nuptial bed.

Following his divorce, Mr. S. sustained a satisfactory sexual relationship with a married woman for four months. Then he contracted influenza. At the end of his illness, the woman came to see him. To his dismay, he found himself for the first time incapable either of desire or erection. For several years thereafter his attempts at sexual relations with women were frustrated by erectile failure or premature ejaculation.

In the year before seeking therapy he had fallen in love with a woman of twenty-four who worked in his office. She reciprocated his feeling, the couple went to bed, and Mr. S. ejaculated prematurely. In spite of this, "he managed to deflorate her." The young woman seemed pleased by the experience, and wishing to avoid spoiling the good effect, Mr. S. desisted from further attempts at coitus with her for six months.

Finally, before she was to go away on a vacation, he tried to have intercourse with her again, and ejaculated before entry. While she was gone, Mr. S. sought to have relations with two other women but couldn't achieve an erection. In desperation, he went to a psychiatrist who injected him with huge doses of testosterone. That this did not help was proved on his sweetheart's return, when further attempts with her ended in failure. Her ardor was, understandably, starting to cool, and it was at this point that he sought therapy.

From the tenth interview on, Mr. S. had the principle of reciprocal inhibition explained to him, and he was also instructed in the techniques of deep relaxation. He was advised to adopt a relaxed attitude toward intercourse. Unless he had a strong erection beforehand, he was told, he was not to attempt coitus, and then he was not to aim solely at some preconceived level of performance.

At the twelfth interview he was hypnotized, relaxed as deeply as possible, and then told to imagine himself in bed with his girl. The therapist's report, unfortunately, shies at revealing what transpired in the interview, beyond this point.

But that the therapy was successful Mr. S. confirmed in the fourteenth interview. He had twice succeeded in having intercourse with his girl friend, he said. The first

time he had been slightly premature, but the second time
he had maintained the erection very well. He was so
heartened by this turn of events that he married the
young woman. Two days after the marriage he reported
that he and his bride had had simultaneous orgasms two
nights in a row.

Over the next six weeks Mr. S., under the therapist's
guidance, consolidated the new pattern of performance
—broken only once by a premature episode when he allowed himself to have intercourse against his inclination.
After twenty-three interviews, and just three months after it had begun, the treatment was terminated. Follow-
ups through five and a half years revealed that Mr. S.
was completely satisfied with his sex life.

A final point with regard to our case histories con-
cerns the presentation of the anxiety-arousing stimuli in
the desensitization process. In all three cases this was
done by verbal suggestion, the patient being asked to
imagine successive objects or situations in the hierarchy.

"It will be apparent, however, says Aubrey Yates,

> that an alternative procedure would be one in which the
> hierarchy consisted of real objects or situations, graded
> according to the amount of anxiety that they aroused.
> The former procedure may be termed imaginal desensiti-
> zation (SD-I); the latter real-life or in vivo disensitiza-
> tion (SD-R). While it might be thought that the natural
> tendency of behavior therapists would be to use the SD-
> R technique, in fact, the vast majority of SD studies have
> utilized the SD-I technique. The principal reason for pre-
> ferring the SD-I technique is, of course, one of economy.
> It is clearly easier to work with complex hierarchies of
> objects and situations if these only have to be visualized
> as opposed to actually setting up real-life situations or
> building objects.

Moreover, the test of any SD technique is its transfer
to real life, and in this, as we have seen, SD-I succeeds.
Yet the use of SD-R techniques is on the increase, according to Yates. Later on, we shall consider a case in
which the treatment of a fetishist was undertaken with
the real objects of the patient's obsession.

A type of reciprocal inhibition called *assertive training* aims to replace ineffective, fear-ridden reactions to other people with responses in which a patient effectively stands up for himself and experiences a sense of satisfaction in social situations.

Typically, the patient is a man or woman who is constantly criticized and ordered about by family, friends, and associates, and who can do little more than retire in a petulant rage, perhaps *think* about what he would like to say or do but rarely actually saying or doing it. Often he has psychosomatic illnesses or a drinking problem—which frequently clears up when he has learned to make assertive responses.

In treating this kind of patient, the behavior therapist points out the emptiness of his fears of other people and encourages him to express his resentments. This is difficult at first, but as he meets more and more demanding situations, a feeling of confidence develops, inhibiting the withdrawal responses which were generated by his anxiety. Imaginal techniques may be used by the therapist, who may also stage psychodramas in which he portrays a feared other, but the course of therapy bears an organic relation to real-life victories.

Sometimes the patient's rapid progress fills him with a hubris which must be checked by the therapist. Obviously there are occasions when assertive behavior has to be limited. Knowledge and prudence dictate how far one can go in telling off the boss. Moreover, a swift and sharp rebuke may increase the patient's sensitivity rather than otherwise. Assertive responses are desirable only as they further the patient's goals in each particular relationship.

CASE HISTORY (Lazarus). Mr. R., thirty-six, unmarried and living with his mother, came to the therapist in a state of anxiety and despair. He worked at a drafting job far beneath his skills and he had no hope of rising out of it. A compulsion to check and recheck everything sapped his energy and efficiency.

Each time he locked a door, he felt compelled to go back several times to be sure it was locked. "At work," he said, ". . . I'll check the scales again and again, and even though I know the detail is correctly mapped, I go over the figure about ten times before I do the next one. Sometimes it nearly drives me mad, but I've just got to go on and on."

Well groomed and pleasant-looking, Mr. R. was poor at social relationships and easily cowed. Although he had a girl friend, he was afraid to marry her because his mother didn't approve of her and had threatened to cut him out of her will if he did. Clearly, he lived under mama's thumb, resented the fact, but was powerless to do anything about it.

In the fifth interview, training in assertive responses was begun and in the sixth training in progressive relaxation. During the eighth interview a psychodrama was enacted in which the therapist played the roles of various threatening figures whom the patient was required to oppose.

Mr. R. walked into the ninth session excitedly announcing, "It's working. Yesterday, for the first time, I stood up to my mother and she got such a shock that she just said nothing. . . . I even asked my boss for a raise. . . ." The therapist expressed his approval and encouraged the patient to practice his new habit of assertive responses.

In the tenth interview a direct attack was made on the checking compulsion. The patient was hypnotized and placed in a deep trance. He was told that he was calm, relaxed, and peaceful. He was to imagine himself drawing a plan, checking his work as he went along. He checked it once, then again. "You begin to check it a third time," the therapist told him, "but now you suddenly feel anxious." Mr. R. writhed, breathing heavily.

The therapist continued: "You leave the plan. You do not check it again. Now you start a new drawing. . . . You are once again calm and relaxed. When I count up to five, you will open your eyes."

The therapist, of course, had been applying the principle of reciprocal inhibition in his treatment of the compulsion, by making the patient feel anxious when he checked too much, whereas before the patient had felt anxious when he did *not* check too much.

The assault on the compulsion via hypnosis continued through the next nine interviews, with transfer to real life affirmed by Mr. R. himself. "I'm turning out five times more work than before. . . . Sometimes I still tend to fuss over things more than I ought to, but that doesn't worry me." The patient's control of his compulsion, of course, increased his confidence, augmenting his ability to make assertive responses; but instruction in the latter still continued.

When the therapist was about twenty minutes late for the twelfth interview, Mr. R. politely but firmly reprimanded—and thus delighted—him; it was something the patient would not have dared do before.

There was a hiatus of five weeks between the nineteenth and twentieth interviews, during which Mr. R. underwent an emergency appendectomy with complications. When he appeared for the twentieth interview, he announced that he had asked his girl friend to marry him, had taken a job in another city, and had arranged for a widowed aunt to live with his mother.

At the twenty-first and final session, Mr. R. came with his fiancée (whom the therapist interviewed privately and found "a sensible person") who showed much confidence in Mr. R. "now that [he] has learned to stand on his own two feet."

After he moved away, the patient maintained contact with the therapist by mail, and once, eight months later, he called him and said, "I have conquered the compulsion for good, and everything is better than I ever expected."

Aversive therapy involves the use of punishment in the presence of unadaptive behavior or related imagery in order to extinguish the behavior. Often the program of treatment is a reciprocally inhibitory one, in that the patient is encouraged to practice incompatible adaptive behavior for which negative or positive reinforcement is given. Aversive therapy—which includes the use of nausea-producing drugs and electric shocks—is obviously an extreme form of behavior conditioning, and it is characteristically resorted to in cases where the patient is difficult to condition and has been, or is likely to be, in trouble with the law.

Aversive therapy has been used in the treatment of transvestism, exhibitionism, and fetishism with notable success and in the treatment of alcoholism and homosexuality with less clear-cut results. Since, as we know from learning theory, the administration of punishment can be hazardous, aversive therapy must be carried out under strict conditions, particularly as regards stimulus-response asynchronism, Eysenck warns. Furthermore, where the patient's neuroticism is high, strong punishment may lead to an increase in anxiety so that the symptoms are worsened rather than extinguished.

Examples of aversive therapy include the use of lists of words relating to the disorder, which "are presented visually and accompanied by shock as the patient reads them aloud." The last word in the list relates to desirable behavior and is presented without a shock. Attempts to overcome homosexual responses have employed drug aversion techniques in combination with the showing of sexually arousing heterosexual films following injections of testosterone to increase libido. Alcoholics have been treated with apomorphine, an aversive drug, in combination with the sight, smell, and taste of whiskey. As often extreme maladaptive behavior is accompanied, and reinforced, by inadequate social responses, aversive therapy may prove to be more effective in combination with training in relaxation and assertiveness. Such a combined program was used with great success in the treatment of a student with a morphine habit whose socialization left much to be desired.

CASE HISTORY (Raymond). A married man of thirty-three was referred to the therapist for consideration of a prefrontal leucotomy after he had attacked a baby carriage.

The patient was in most respects normal. He was intelligent, heterosexual, with no psychotic disorders.

Married, with two children, he was said to be a good husband and father. He worked at a job requiring mechanical skill and ingenuity as well as personal contact, and his employers thought well of him.

In September, 1954, he was haled into court by a woman for smearing oil on her baby carriage, certainly no great crime. What disturbed the authorities in the case, however, was that the man had a history of attacking baby carriages (and pocketbooks as well), and that if unchecked, his fetishistic compulsion might prove dangerous to life and limb. The following incidents were known to the police.

In 1948, while in the RAF, the man was arrested for slashing and setting afire two empty baby carriages in a railway station. He subsequently admitted being responsible for five other incidents of pram-slashing, which the police had been investigating over a period of months. He was convicted of malicious damage, discharged from the service, and put on probation conditional to his accepting medical treatment. He was placed in a mental hospital, where he was diagnosed as being potentially dangerous and unresponsive to psychotherapy. Nevertheless, he was released after only two months.

In early 1950 he smeared a woman's handbag with mucus and scratched and cut up a baby carriage. Following these incidents, he was again hospitalized, this time for sixteen months.

In April, 1952, he drove his motorcycle toward a woman with a baby carriage, swerving at the last moment but still scraping and damaging the vehicle. He was charged with and fined for reckless driving. Four months later, he was convicted of causing malicious damage and fined after he squirted oil on a perambulator and on the skirt and stockings of the woman behind it.

The year before his present trouble he had again come to the attention of the police by driving his motorcycle through a puddle and splashing a woman and her baby carriage with mud.

Although the authorities knew of only these twelve

perambulator attacks, the patient admitted to the therapist that the actual number of such attacks was considerably larger. In most weeks he would make an average of two or three, and on some single days he had damaged several carriages. In the case of pocketbooks, he was usually satisfied to scratch them with a fingernail. Because this could be done unobtrusively, his handbag fetish had led him into difficulty with the law only once. Neither his attacks on pocketbooks nor on baby carriages brought him to orgasm, although they aroused him sexually and resulted in a lessening of tension. But he masturbated to fantasies of these fetish objects and could have coitus with his wife only with the aid of such fantasies.

The patient seemed created for depth therapy; the trouble was he had already had many hours of psychoanalysis, in the course of which he had learned that handbags and baby carriages were "symbolic sexual containers." This had failed to do him any good as far as his compulsion was concerned, and he entered behavior therapy in a state of hopelessness and dejection.

The aversive therapy was SD-R; the patient was shown a collection of handbags and baby carriages, and colored pictures of both after he had received an injection of apomorphine and just before the onset of nausea. This treatment was given every two hours, day and night, for a solid week. Amphetamine was used to keep him awake at night.

At the end of the week he was permitted to go home. He returned to therapy eight days later, reporting that for the first time he had been able to have intercourse with his wife without resorting to his fantasies.

The treatment was resumed, as before. When the emetic effect of the apomorphine lessened, emetine hydrochloride was used in its place. Between treatments, the patient was asked to write an essay on the attractive qualities of baby carriages and handbags. This he did, along with an account of the ways these objects were commonly misused. He was now made to see the pride that he had taken in his eccentricity, the element of exhibitionism it contained, and the threat it represented to his liberty. By the fifth day, just the sight of pocketbooks and baby carriages made him sick.

At this point the treatments began to be given at irregular intervals, while the patient was confined to bed surrounded by the objects of his fetish. By the ninth day, he was sobbing uncontrollably, repeating over and over, "Take them away."

The weeping continued until the objects were removed from his sight, and he was given a glass of milk and a sedative. The next day he voluntarily surrendered a collection of photo negatives of baby carriages, which he said he had carried with him for years.

He left the hospital shortly thereafter and continued as an outpatient for six months. Then he was readmitted for a booster treatment. This consisted of aversive drugs used in conjunction with a color movie of women pushing baby carriages and carrying handbags in ways which he had theretofore found provoking. Each time a wave of nausea overcame him, the film was started up, and it was continued until the nausea subsided.

A follow-up nineteen months after therapy was begun disclosed that he had had no further trouble with the police. The patient himself reported that he no longer masturbated to the old fantasies, nor were they necessary to his having sexual relations with his wife. The latter confirmed that their love life had "greatly improved" and that she was no longer worrying about his being taken away by the police. At his place of employment the patient had won a promotion. His probation officer declared that "very noticeable progress had been made. . . . His general attitude to life, his conversation, and his appearance have all shown marked improvement."

At first glance, the notion that repeating maladaptive behavior can bring about its extinction doesn't seem to make much sense. But if we recall Guthrie's story of the little girl who gave up lighting matches after she had set afire more than she cared to, the principle of *negative practice* will appear worthy of investigation. Guthrie's exemplary tale is confirmed in more scientific terms by Pavlov and Hull, who noted that the practice of a response, even with reinforcement, could lead to its extinction.

Negative practice, indeed, grew out of various criticisms of Watson's law of frequency, particularly those of Knight Dunlap. In contradiction of Watson, Dunlap postulated "that repetition has no effect on the probable recurrence of a response except insofar as certain other factors operate through it." In practical therapeutic terms this has come to mean that a response can, so to speak, be made to wear itself out if it is continually elicited with the purpose of causing its extinction.

In one of the earliest tests of Dunlap's postulate, G. Wakeman "attempted to eliminate certain habitual errors [he made] in piano selections from Bach's 'Toccata and Fugue in D Minor.' He practiced the selections for two weeks with the wrong notes deliberately inserted. On the fifteenth day he played the pieces without error, and, after several errorless performances, called in a pupil for a demonstration of his success—only to find that the errors reappeared."

What had apparently gone wrong was that Wakeman had not taken into account the factor of an audience in his performance difficulties. Factors that sustain unwanted behavior as a tension-relieving device must be removed for negative practice to work. This is the real meaning of Dunlap's principle, which we see illustrated in the following case involving treatment of a stutterer along negative practice lines.

CASE HISTORY (Case). A man of thirty-two stuttered by repeating whole phrases: "Boy, do I—boy, do I— boy, do I—boy, do I—boy, do I get seasick." Or his vocalization might come out "Boy—boy—boy—do I get seasick."

The stuttering had appeared when he was seven years old. He had fallen on his head the year before, and both his parents and he attributed his disability to this accident. While stuttering, his diaphragm constricted and his breath became short; at particularly bad times he would turn very red or even purple. He was always extremely tense and trembly when talking.

He lived at home with his parents and held an insignificant job at a large company. His father, fifty-four, was neurotic and irritable and constantly belittled the young man and his friends. His mother, forty-eight, "invariably complained of a weak heart or a nervous headache whenever something did not please her. She managed to keep the boy from marrying by convincing him she would die if he left home."

Although "intensely asocial," the patient had a male friend with whom he often went sailing, usually becoming seasick in the process, and several girl friends whom he dated irregularly. He was especially jealous of one girl he claimed to be engaged to, though he rarely saw her.

A program of negative practice of the speech problem was instituted with good results during the practice hour, but with indifferent results outside. After four weeks, it became apparent to the therapist that the program would have to be expanded to include an attack on the factors that supported the unadaptive behavior.

The patient was advised to spend more time with friends with whom he shared common interests and less and less time under his mother's influence. He was also encouraged to cultivate the friendship of a young woman whose company he found congenial. At the same time, he was trained in making assertive responses. This resulted in "a clash with his father, in which he won equal rights. Then, when a similar clash with his mother proved that she did not die from shock (although she did produce an apparent nervous prostration), he gained a measure of self-confidence in his home and in his vocational life," winning a minor promotion in his company. Because he was a suggestible person, the therapist was able to persuade him that his seasickness would now disappear—which, with one exceptional episode, proved to be the case.

In the meantime, negative practice continued for nine

months, including three one-month rest periods, being given twice a week for one-hour periods. In the last sessions practice was enforced by electric shock.

Following the young man's social and vocational adjustment, improvement came quickly. One year after conclusion of the course of therapy, the patient was followed up by the therapist and judged to be mentally and emotionally more balanced, with little or no trouble with his speech.

Negative practice is sometimes confused with what is called *impulsive therapy* or *flooding,* to which it bears a superficial resemblance. Implosive therapy is an upside-down reversal of systematic desensitization in which the most noxious stimulus in the hierarchy is presented first —either in imagination or in vivo—and repeatedly "in massed practice from which escape is impossible. . . ."

"Essentially," says Yates, "flooding or implosive therapy represents a form of forced reality testing; that is, if the subject is prevented from making his usual avoidance response to reduce anxiety generated by the CS, and if in fact, the anticipated traumatic event does not occur, then the conditioned anxiety will extinguish, since it is no longer reinforced by drive reduction resulting from the avoidance response."

Reviewing the literature on implosive therapy, Wolpe tells of one experiment in which an adolescent girl with a fear of automobiles was placed by force in the back of a car and driven continuously for four hours. The phobia reached hysterical heights, but then receded, and at the end of the ride was permanently gone. In another case (Gerz), a woman of twenty-nine with multiple fears—of supermarkets, of cars and subways, of being alone, of eating in restaurants (because she might vomit), and of heights—sought treatment of her behavior problems.

She was instructed to try to bring about whatever she was afraid would happen to her. She was to try to vomit while dining out with her husband and friends and create the greatest possible mess. She was to drive to markets, hairdressers and banks "trying to get as panicky as possible." In six weeks she had lost her fears in her home situation, and shortly thereafter drove all by herself to [her therapist's] office, about five miles from her home. Four months later, she drove with her husband to New York City, a hundred miles from home, across the George Washington Bridge, back through the Lincoln Tunnel, and attended a goodbye party on the lower deck of an ocean liner. [The therapist] states that two years later she was free of symptoms.

Despite such reported successes, implosive therapy has been criticized for being likely to generate more anxiety than the patient can handle and thereby to exacerbate the fear response. Indeed, the results produced by emotional flooding have been conflicting and contradictory, and Wolpe considers the procedure "a final recourse, to be taken after every other measure has failed." The parent who hurls kicking, screaming, and hydrophobic little Johnny off the dock and into the water to teach him how to swim is practicing a form of implosive therapy. Sometimes Johnny does learn how to swim; but sometimes he learns to dread the water even more—and his well-meaning parent into the bargain. Obviously, the variables under which implosive therapy is given need to be better understood and controlled before this form of behavior therapy is undertaken without hazard.

From the principle of the Skinner box and its various reinforcement schedules has evolved a class of procedures known as *operant therapy*. Operant therapy involves reciprocal inhibition but differs from the techniques that we have considered in one essential respect. It does not attempt to elicit responses, which are then rewarded or punished. It allows the subject behavior to be freely emitted and then presents consequences which may reinforce, extinguish, or modify the behavior, or shape it into new forms. The patient is then "free" to repeat or alter the behavior in light of the consequences he has learned it will produce.

A concrete example will highlight this difference. In Raymond's case of the man who had a baby carriage fetish, aversive stimuli were presented in conjunction with real carriages and pictures of carriages in a program that turned the objects of the fetish into objects to be avoided. Once assenting to the program, the patient had no further control of it but had to submit passively to the stimuli with which he was bombarded by the therapist until he literally cried stop. In a sense he was in a Skinner box but without the manipulandum.

A counterpart of this case, conducted along operant lines, is reported by Feldman and McCullough. The patient—or patients, since the procedure was used with eight different subjects—was a male homosexual seeking to change his sexual orientation to a heterosexual one. Pictures of attractive men were projected on a screen, followed eight seconds later by an electric shock. But the patient had a manipulandum in the form of a switch with which he could turn off the picture on the screen before the eight seconds had elapsed and thus avoid the shock. Later the switching response became effective only intermittently. The therapists "also presented pictures of attractive females on some trials continuous with the removal of the male. When the picture of the female had been removed . . . the patient could obtain its return (on a random schedule) by pressing a switch. Since the absence of a female picture meant that a picture of a male (with the shock contingency) might reappear, the response of re-presenting the female pictures constituted a further extension of the avoidance procedure." As a result of this treatment, a majority of the patients reported that they had given up homosexual practices and become more interested in heterosexual ones.

In the above experiment, the desired response was evoked by negative reinforcement of the heterosexual choices in conjunction with punishment of the homosexual ones. But positive reinforcement is as commonly used in operant therapy, where the response is in the patient's repertoire but is weak or recessive. In the case of a mute retarded girl, vocal responses were established by reinforcing any vocalization which the child emitted.

The girl, however, stopped vocalizing when the therapist answered her. Recognizing her sensitivity to his voice, the therapist at first spoke softly enough not to silence the girl, then gradually raised the level of his voice and the number of his vocalizations until his normal speech ceased to have the inhibiting effect. Thereafter reinforcement was required only when the girl vocalized shortly after the therapist had.

In another case, positive reinforcement was used to increase the rate of eating by a patient with anorexia by a variety of environmental reinforcers such as his being given magazines, being allowed to watch television shows, and being presented with visitors whenever he ingested food.

A thirteen-year-old boy who had never displayed appropriate toilet behavior was finally trained by positive reinforcement, which consisted of free time away from his ward when he eliminated in the bowl or when his clothing was found to be clean during periodic checks.

Response costs is the name given to a form of operant conditioning in which a pleasurable stimulus is withdrawn when the behavior emitted is undesired and re-presented when desired behavior is emitted in its place.

In one experiment, three young children who were thumb-suckers were shown a movie cartoon. The film was stopped each time one of them thrust his thumb in his mouth, and it was resumed in the absence of thumb sucking. In this group the rate of thumb sucking was greatly reduced in comparison with a control group which was allowed to watch the cartoon without a response cost for its thumb sucking. A parallel case involved a man with multiple tics, who was allowed to listen to music continuously if the tics did not occur more often than at 1½-second intervals; if they occurred more frequently, the music was interrupted. This technique produced a greater reduction in the number of tics than the playing of the music without any interruptions.

The cases just described are typical of many others cited in a recent survey of operant therapy techniques by Sherman and Bauer. That they differ from the kinds of cases—the classic phobias and obsessions—treated by S-R reciprocal inhibition procedures may have occurred to the reader. Operant therapy is apparently practiced on a primitive level largely in institutional settings, in schools and hospitals, where an attack can be made on unadaptive behavior as it is emitted in the course of day-to-day living. That operant therapy has not achieved a firm foothold in the consulting room is probably due less to its limitations than to the fact that the training of therapists in its techniques is still far from widespread. Such training is also technically complex and difficult. The case of operant treatment of the homosexual patients, however, shows that this type of behavior therapy can be adapted to the office setting.

In this chapter it has been possible only to suggest the range of techniques that are today being employed by behavior therapists. That these techniques will be refined and further perfected with increasing experimentation cannot be doubted. Having freed themselves from the psychodynamic assumptions that all therapists formerly used, behavior therapists are forging in other directions. One direction will undoubtedly be the application of the findings of cybernetics and ethology in the treatment of behavior disorders. Both of these sciences lie outside the realm of learning theory but supplement it in different ways. While learning theory has been, and is likely to remain, the chief basis of behavior therapy, the latter has never embraced a closed system in the way the psychodynamic therapies have. In this sense it is truly dynamic—open to criticism and change and responsive to the challenges that an increasingly complex and demanding world is likely to bring.

Part Four:

LOOKING FORWARD

Each wave of theoretical advance from pure research anticipates a spurt of growth in engineering, for each makes possible a new technology, which sires, in turn, new offspring of its own.

PERRY LONDON (1969)

Chapter Seven

Human Engineering

Behavioral Techniques in Society

The application of behavioral techniques to large groups of people is nothing new. Most of the laws which rule our lives work along behavioral lines to some degree. If you pay your taxes, you can enjoy the services and protections of our society (reinforcement); if you don't, you will be subject to legal prosecution and may be fined and even imprisoned (punishment). If you are imprisoned, acceptable behavior will usually produce an easing of your penalties, possibly culminating in a restoration of your freedom (withdrawal of negative reinforcement).

These applications are so widely known, used, and accepted that they arouse little opposition. Sometimes, of course, they fail to work as well as they should theoretically. During the Vietnam war, numerous persons refused to pay their income tax because the benefits of compliance as well as the punishments for noncompliance with the law seemed to them outweighed by the destruction of life and property which their money would pay for. Still, the income tax system did not break down, because there was enough assent to keep it working, and the war wound down eventually. The case of the Prohibition Amendment was somewhat different: here the breaking of the law, combined with its nonenforcement, was so widespread that the behavioral machinery set up to keep it operative began to run in reverse and finally had to be jettisoned.

Although we are inured to living with many kinds of behavior controls, the thought of human engineering sends a chill down the spine of many of us—and not without reason. Knowledge of what a modern despotic government can do, using behavioral techniques, to enforce its rules of behavior, is present to us all. The ghastly visions of Huxley's *Brave New World* and Orwell's *1984*, in which human beings have become totally controlled automatons, are real enough to warn us that our rights and liberties are as fragile and perishable as they are precious.

Yet it is the proposition of this book that the laws of behavior are neutral, like all laws of nature; that they are only good or bad in how we use them; and whether they help to usher in a nightmare era or a golden age of peace and stability depends on ourselves. One thing seems certain: whether or not we accept the challenges of the laws of behavior in a positive way, behavior management techniques will become an increasing feature of our lives, because they work to hold the fabric of society together better than any other techniques we have.

Let us look at the possibilities. Basically, there are three.

In the Soviet Union, human engineering became an early concern of the revolutionary government. Having just thrown off the oppressive yoke of the tsars, the Soviets set out to create a new society in which the lowliest worker and peasant would be the equal of any king. Their main problem was that, by supplanting the tsar and church, the Soviets had also removed the authorities which had given individual behavior its legitimacy.

A minority party, they had seized political control by force and without popular assent. To keep themselves in power, they proclaimed the myth that their rule would only be temporary, and then they proceeded to engineer the assent they lacked. This was one of the reasons they were so interested in the experimental work of Pavlov and his associates, whose discoveries promised to bring them greater control of their population.

The Soviet Union became the biggest behavioral science laboratory the world has yet seen. From birth to old age, every citizen's behavior became the state's concern. Docile behavior was reinforced and unacceptable behavior brought either nonreinforcement or outright punishment. In the beginning, the methods used were sometimes brutal, and many a recalcitrant died before a firing squad or amid the ice and snow of Siberia. But as more sophisticated and effective behavior controls came into being, such crude measures were dispensed with. Managing and publishing all information, dispensing all the material goods and benefits available in its lands, the Soviet state has achieved as absolute a control over the behavior of its citizens as any Roman tyrant might have wished for.

A few facets of behavior management in the Soviet Union have brought benefits. Medical and old-age assistance are available to all; schooling is free to the highest levels of education in accordance with individual ability; social violence is minimal.

Although human engineering has its frightful aspect, it has continued to exert a fascination upon people who seek a world more rationally organized and controllable than the one we live in today.

B. F. Skinner, in a novel entitled *Walden Two,** offers a second approach to behavior management in society. Walden Two is less like Walden One than Brook Farm; that is, it is an intentional community organized along Fourieristic socialist lines by like-minded people who wish to improve the quality of their lives and the lives of their children. It differs from the Soviet model in that management of behavior is in the hands not of the state but of the members of the community, although the basic structure of the community has been set up by one man, its founder.

---

* I am probably not the first to question the appropriateness of this title or whatever possessed Skinner to use it, since Walden One was not set up by Thoreau to be a community or even an alternative life-style. It was an individual experience or experiment, which Thoreau ended after it had served his various *personal* purposes.

It differs also from most present-day rural hippie communes in three important respects. There is no retreat to primitive industry (candle-making, hand weaving, and the like), which Skinner feels is inefficient and enslaving to the individual; on the contrary, the most advanced production methods, consonant with the goals of the society, are sought. There is no hard-and-fast separation from the larger outside world, with which Walden Two exchanges goods and services. And the community exists in a spirit of rigid experimentation—a characteristic which seems more in keeping with the author than with what we know of such communities in real life.

The keynote of Walden Two, however, is that its laws are not sustained by force or the threat of force (aspects of punishment) but by positive reinforcement.

In one of the best-argued passages of the book, the founder of the community, a man named Frazier, explains the superiority of this principle.

> The old school made the amazing mistake of supposing that . . . by removing a situation a person likes or setting up one he doesn't like—in other words by punishing him—it was possible to reduce the probability that he would behave in a given way again. That simply doesn't hold. . . . [Force is] temporarily effective, that's the worst of it. That explains several thousand years of bloodshed. Even nature has been fooled. We instinctively punish a person who doesn't behave as we like—we spank him if he's a child or strike him if he's a man. A nice distinction! The immediate effect of the blow teaches us to strike again. Retribution and revenge are the most natural things on earth. But in the long run the man we strike is no less likely to repeat his act. . . .
>
> Now that we know how positive reinforcement works and why negative doesn't . . . we can be more deliberate and hence more successful, in our cultural design. We can achieve a sort of control under which the controlled, though they are following a code much more scrupulously than was ever the case under the old system, nevertheless *feel free*. They are doing what they want to do, not what they are forced to do. That's the source of the tremendous power of positive reinforcement—there's no restraint and no revolt. . . .

Skinner has obviously thought hard about what the ideal human community should be like, and many aspects of Walden Two are worthy of serious consideration. There is complete equality of the sexes in all things. Men and women marry and mate in their late teens, thus averting sexual frustration and its consequences. When the women are in their twenties, they have finished bearing all the children they are likely to want and they then take up personal goals. Babies are raised in communal nurseries, in which the mothers may work as they choose. The children grow up equally in an atmosphere of care and concern, free of envy, strife, shock, competition, and punishment. They go to work early, but work in Walden Two is inseparable from education and, in any case, because of efficiencies which have been engineered, is not onerous. There is much leisure in Walden Two—to act in or attend plays, to perform in or hear orchestral ensembles.

Members of the community who wish to pursue higher learning in universities and graduate and professional schools are free to leave to do so, with the understanding that the benefits of their training will accrue to the community. While the happiness of the individual is a prime consideration of Walden Two, the highest ethic is a communal one. The individual growing up there learns that his well-being is inseparable from that of the group as a whole.

Skinner conceives of Walden Two not only as an experiment to exist in isolation but as something germinal which will grow and spread as the health, efficiency, and successful engineering of human behavior become recognized by the population at large.

In one of the final chapters of *Walden Two*, Frazier and a humanist philosopher named Castle have a heated debate about behavior control vs. freedom.

"Mr. Castle," said Frazier very earnestly, "let me ask you a question. I warn you, it will be the most terrifying question of your life. *What would you do if you found yourself in possession of an effective science of behav-*

ior? Suppose you suddenly found it possible to control the behavior of men as you wished. What would you do? . . .

"What would I do?" said Castle thoughtfully. "I think I would dump your science of behavior in the ocean."

"And deny men all the help you could otherwise give them?"

"And give them the freedom they would otherwise lose forever!"

"How could you give them freedom?"

"By refusing to control them."

"But you would only be leaving the control in other hands."

"Whose?"

"The charlatan, the demagogue, the salesman, the ward heeler, the bully, the cheat, the educator, the priest —all who are now in possession of the techniques of behavioral engineering."

"A pretty good share of the control would remain in the hands of the individual himself."

Castle's answer is not satisfactory to Frazier (nor, presumably, to Skinner), who argues that the idea of behavioral engineering is inimical to any notion of individual freedom; that you can't have the one and continue to believe in the other. But this is an argument that rests on soft ground, since paradox is not unknown to science, and it admits a third approach to human engineering.

This is an approach based on *awareness*. As elucidated by Perry London, this approach lacks the certainty and efficiency of the Soviet system or of Walden Two but leaves in the individual's hands the element of choice. Or the illusion of choice? Skinner is undoubtedly right in declaiming that our actions are manipulated to a greater degree than we acknowledge by politicians, salesmen, and the like; but awareness of such control and of the way it operates gives us—in a democratic society, at least—a means to break or circumvent it if we don't like it. And awareness of the techniques of behavioral engineering gives us a positive instrument for creating the kinds of behavior we wish to have.

One of London's most interesting demonstrations of awareness is a piece of hindsight involving the change of the status of women in modern society. Although the traditional role of women was hemmed about with all manner of pieties, religious, moral, and romantic, it depended upon the negative reinforcement of their punishment for sexual transgression. For centuries, a woman who became pregnant outside of marriage also became an outcast; she suffered social opprobrium, a loss of rights, and economic disabilities which endured as long as she lived, or until she got a man to marry her. With marriage, negative reinforcers were withdrawn. Then she was positively reinforced to have children and spend her life caring for them. Her role was predetermined by behavior controls, regardless of how free the society she lived in thought itself to be.

The problem for a woman who did not wish this role was how to gain control of her body. Of course many women did not perceive the problem in these terms. In the nineteenth century, for instance, the solution was thought to lie in a combination of temperance and voting rights. Even those who understood the matter more clearly were hampered by lack of a device that would take control out of the hands of society and give it to women themselves. Such contraceptives as existed (1) were not entirely reliable and (2) were in the control of men. With the development of the pill, these last two barriers to women's liberation came down, and the New Woman was born.

What is so extraordinary about the pill is that its consequences were foreseen by few people because there was little awareness of the complex of behavioral restraints which it destroyed. Indeed, at first the pill was welcomed only for its convenience and for letting sexual partners enjoy themselves freely. If social consequences were thought of, it was in terms of population control in far-off Asia and South America.

Hardly anyone foresaw the consequences the pill would have in changing not only the status of women but also of marriage, the family, and the roles of men. Yet these results might have been predicted to an extent by anyone aware of the behavioral forces at work in the total situation.

From hindsight there is only a step to foresight. We need not leave ourselves at the mercy of the "future shocks" which scientific advances bring, any more than we need to submit to the manipulation of tyrants. Both accord with the laws of learning, which also hold that new learning is always possible. If, for example, the pill has wreaked havoc with the traditional family, we as individuals still have the choice of passively welcoming the death of the family or designing new behavioral structures which give it new support and life.

Obviously, the old system of negatively reinforcing the female—which was totally inequitable and never worked well, besides—has to be abandoned forever. If we decide that the family is a value that should be preserved, then new positive reinforcers of both the male and female roles will have to be set up. But it may be that alternatives to the family will seem more feasible: many life experiments in this direction are already under way. Whatever, in the long run, appears to be best, the laws of learning give us a means of fostering and maintaining.

A Glossary of Terms

assertive training—training in the outward expression of normal feelings, by which the anxiety that inhibits such expression is reciprocally weakened or extinguished.

aversive therapy—therapy in which unadaptive behavior is conditioned to punishment in order to extinguish it.

boundary conditions—conditions that must be present in order that a theory be applicable in a given situation.

cathexis—a learned tendency to seek certain goals in preference to others when experiencing a particular drive.

classical conditioning—a type of learning in which the response originally elicited by one of two stimuli presented together is elicited by the other. See *conditioned stimulus, conditioned response, unconditioned stimulus, unconditioned response*.

cognitive map—an organism's concept of its life space and the objects in it.

conditioned inhibition—a habit of not responding to a stimulus that previously elicited a response.

conditioned response—a response to a conditioned stimulus.

conditioned stimulus—a previously neutral stimulus that is capable of eliciting a response by having been paired with an unconditioned stimulus.

continuous reinforcement—a schedule of reinforcement in which a reinforcer follows each response.

counter-conditioning—see *reciprocal inhibition*.

cue—a stimulus that is distinctive enough to determine the type of response and the time and place of its occurrence.

discrimination—the learned ability to make appropriate responses to different but similar stimuli.

drive—any aroused state of an organism, such as hunger, thirst, sex, pain, etc.

dysthymia—neuroticism of the introverted personality, characterized by anxieties, phobias, compulsions, etc.

equivalence belief—a learned belief that a symbol of reward or punishment is equivalent to the reward or punishment and therefore in itself rewarding or punishing.

excitation—any act or process by which a reflex is evoked.

extinction—the weakening or elimination of the tendency to make a response; in behavior therapy, specifically the elimination of an unadaptive response.

extravert—a type of individual who tends to be outgoing, voluble, and persistent, and who characteristically is unable to form quick and strong conditioned responses.

field cognition modes—ways of learning or tendencies to learn certain things about a situation rather than other things.

field expectancies—an organism's knowledge about how the world looks, feels, smells, tastes, and sounds, and how its parts relate to each other.

flooding—see *implosive therapy*.

fractional antedating reaction—an anticipatory response to a situation in which reinforcement regularly occurs.

generalization—the tendency of a response to occur to a new stimulus similar to one that was present when the response was learned.

habit—a learned tendency to respond to certain stimuli in a fixed or regular way.

hysteria—see *psychopathy*.

implosive therapy—a therapeutic procedure in which the patient is exposed to an intense anxiety-evoking stimulus from which he cannot escape until the stimulus loses its power to evoke anxiety.

incentive motivation—the tendency of large rewards to raise levels of performance higher than small rewards.

inhibition—any act or process by which a response is restrained.

instrumental conditioning—a type of learning that serves the purpose of attaining reward or escaping punishment.

intermittent reinforcement—a schedule of reinforcement in which a reinforcer follows some responses but not others.

intervening variable—a hypothetical variable that mediates between stimulus and response.

introvert—a type of individual who tends to be thoughtful, quiet, and considerate, and who characteristically is easily and well conditioned.

latent learning—learning that takes place despite the absence of a response to a stimulus.

manipulandum—that part of a Skinner box which, when manipulated by the subject, results in the delivery of a reinforcer.

negative practice—the repetition of behavior for the purpose of extinguishing it.

negative reinforcement—an event whose removal following a response strengthens the tendency of that response to occur; also synonymous with punishment.

negative reinforcer—see *negative reinforcement*.

operant—an item of operant behavior.

operant behavior—behavior that operates upon the environment and produces consequences.

operant therapy—therapy involving procedures by which behavior as emitted is reinforced, shaped, or extinguished.

oscillation—the tendency of performance to rise or fall in a seemingly random manner.

primary drive—see *drive*.

primary reinforcement—see *reinforcement*.

primary reinforcer—see *reinforcement*.

psychopathy—neuroticism of the extraverted personality, characterized by aggression and asocial behavior.

reactive inhibition—the tendency of a response to decrease when it is elicited repeatedly.

reciprocal inhibition—the principle of behavior therapy according to which an adaptive response incompatible with an unadaptive one is induced in the presence of the stimuli that evoke the latter in order to weaken the bond between those stimuli and the latter.

reinforcement—an event which, when following a response, strengthens the tendency of that response to reoccur.

reinforcer—see *reinforcement*.

respondent behavior—reflexive behavior; behavior that is elicited by specific stimuli and subject to classic conditioning.

response—any item of behavior.

response costs—a type of operant therapy in which a pleasurable stimulus is withdrawn when the behavior emitted is undesired and re-presented when desired behavior is emitted in its place.

scalloping—a pattern of response in which the rate is lowest after a reinforcer is received and then gradually increases.

schedule of reinforcement—the schedule according to which reinforcers are delivered to the subject in a Skinner box. See *continuous reinforcement* and *intermittent reinforcement*.

secondary conditioning—conditioning in which a conditioned stimulus is presented with a neutral one and a response to the latter alone is then elicited.

secondary drive—the tendency of a neutral stimulus that has been paired with a drive to be arousing.

secondary reinforcement—the tendency of a neutral stimulus that has been paired with a reinforcer to reinforce a response.

secondary reinforcer—see *secondary reinforcement*.

shaping—the fashioning of new patterns of behavior by reinforcing some responses and not reinforcing others.

Skinner box—a box or room containing a manipulandum and a means for delivering reinforcers.

spontaneous recovery—the tendency of a response that has been extinguished to recover with the passage of time and without further training.

stimulus—any sensation, significant in that it controls or elicits a response.

superstitious behavior—behavior that recurs following reinforcement that is delivered without regard to its occurrence.

systematic desensitization—a therapeutic process by which an unadaptive response is broken down by the presentation of successively stronger stimuli while the response is in a state of inhibition.

threshold—the point on the performance scale where minimum performance is observable.

unconditioned response—an unlearned response.

unconditioned stimulus—a stimulus capable of eliciting an unlearned response.

Chapter Notes

Preface

The quotation of Perry London is from *Behavior Control*, p. 234. B. F. Skinner's discussion of freedom as an illusion is to be found in Chapter 2, "Freedom," of *Beyond Freedom and Dignity*.

Chapter One

There are many accounts of the way Freudian and other psychodynamic systems work. A good single source is Donald H. Ford and Hugh B. Urban's *Systems of Psychotherapy*. Aubrey J. Yates in *Behavior Therapy* cites R. W. White's description of the Little Hans case, pp. 8–9, and details the attack on psychodynamic psychology, including Eysenck's study, pp. 3–13. The experiments of Jones and of Mowrer and Mowrer are described by Richard M. Suinn in *Fundamentals of Behavior Pathology*, pp. 24–25.

Chapter Two

Cyril M. Franks in "Behavior Therapy and Its Pavlovian Origins" cites a number of early applications of behavioral techniques, pp. 4–6. The quoted characterization of Sechenev is his, p. 6. Biographical details relating to Sechenev are from Robert I. Watson, *The Great Psychologists from Aristotle to Freud*, p. 408. The discussion of Sechenev's ideas is derived mainly from Gregory A. Kimble, *Foundations of Conditioning and Learning*, pp. 12–17, and to a lesser extent, from Gregory Razran, *Mind in Evolution*, p. 10, both of whom cite Sechenev's writings. The section on Pavlov closely follows Watson, *op. cit.*, pp. 408–412, whence comes the unattributed quotation (p. 411). The quote on the relation between massed practice and inhibition occurs in D. C. Kendrick, "The Theory of Conditioned Inhibition," p. 222. Pavlov's statements are from citations in Razran, *op. cit.*, p. 11. Kimble's explanation of Pavlov's theory is in Kimble, *op. cit.,* p. 35. The five causes of neurosis are mentioned by Franks, *op. cit.,* p. 8.

My discussion of John B. Watson and his ideas relies mainly on Winfred Hill, *Learning,* pp. 32–40, in which the cited description of walking appears (p. 36). R. I. Watson, *op. cit.,* quotes Watson's "manifesto," p. 406. Watson and Rayner's report on their experiments with Little Albert is titled "Conditioned Emotional Reactions"; the citations are taken directly from it, *passim.*

Hill, *op. cit.,* pp. 40–55, is the chief source for the section on Guthrie and, specifically, for the unattributed quotation (p. 48). The citation of Hilgard and Bower, as well as Guthrie's "reply," appears in *Theories of Learning,* p. 104.

Chapter Three

Winfred Hill, *Learning,* pp. 57–58, describes Thorndike's cat-in-the-cage experiment and his conclusions about it. The discussion of the law of effect and its history, including Thorndike's statements, is drawn from Hardy C. Wilcoxon, "Introduction to the Problem of Reinforcement," pp. 10–21. Wilcoxon's critical quote appears on pp. 17–18. The explanation of behavior as drive reductionism, according to Hull, is from Wilcoxon, *op. cit.,* pp. 35–36. Hull's engineer's outlook is noted by Hill, *op. cit.,* p. 129. Wilcoxon, *op. cit.,* discusses Hull's relation to Newton, pp. 33–34, and cites the marginal notes (p. 33). The discussion of Hull's method follows Hill, *op. cit.,* pp. 129–135. Eysenck's quotation is found in his article, "Modern Learning Theory," p. 80.

Hill explains Hull's later incorporation of incentive motivation and provides the revised formula for performance, *op. cit.,* pp. 136–138. The material on responsive and reactive inhibition is also drawn from Hill, *ibid.,* pp. 140–141, but the formulas accounting for them are from Eysenck, *op. cit.,* pp. 80–81, as is the quote on Gwynne Jones's revision (p. 81). The balance of the section follows Hill, *op. cit.,* pp. 139–145, and Hill's final evaluative statement is found there on p. 156.

The discussion of Skinner basically follows Hill's excellent treatment of Skinner, *op. cit.,* pp. 60–79, as well as, to a lesser extent, Wilcoxon, *op. cit.,* pp. 29–32, where Skinner's comment on Pavlov occurs (p. 30). Hill's statement on man's beliefs is found on pp. 54–75, *op. cit.*

Chapter Four

Again, Winfred Hill's *Learning,* pp. 114–128, offers the best brief discussion of Tolman's system; and this, together with

Wilcoxon, "Introduction to the Problem of Reinforcement," pp. 27–28, and Hilgard and Bower, *Theories of Learning,* pp. 213–217, is followed here. The two unattributed quotations are from Wilcoxon, *op. cit.,* p. 28, and Hilgard and Bower, *op. cit.,* p. 214, respectively.

Chapter Five

The first part of this chapter follows H. J. Eysenck's excellent essay, "Learning Theory and Behavior Therapy," pp. 4–21, in which occur the various quotations attributed to him. Aubrey J. Yates, *Behavior Therapy,* makes the distinction between mono- and polysymptomatic abnormalities (p. 60) and is also the source for material on behavioral treatment of psychotics (pp. 288–291). The quotation from Franks occurs in "Individual Differences in Conditioning and Associated Techniques," p. 162. The discussion of language as an elicitor of behavior follows Perry London, *Behavior Control,* pp. 109–112. The excerpt by Andrew Salter is from "The Theory and Practice of Conditioned Reflex Therapy," pp. 32–33. Joseph Wolpe provides the statistical information relative to the duration and success of behavior therapy in "The Comparative Clinical Status of Conditioning Therapies and Psychoanalysis," pp. 14–15. D. Walton's discussion of his patient with neuro-dermatitis occurs in "The Application of Learning Theory to the Treatment of a Case of Neuro-Dermatitis," pp. 272–274.

Chapter Six

Joseph Wolpe's experiments with the cats is described in Wolpe's "Reciprocal Inhibition as the Main Basis of Psychotherapeutic Effects," pp. 89–90. Albert Bandura, "Psychotherapy as a Learning Process," points to the foreign origins of the leading behavior therapists, p. 339, referred to in the footnote. The case history of the tram driver is found in Wolpe. *op. cit.,* p. 109. Carol M's case history is described in A. A. Lazarus, "The Elimination of Children's Phobias by Deconditioning," pp. 116–118. The list of patient fears, as well as the therapist's breakdown of it, may be found in Wolpe, *The Practice of Behavior Therapy,* p. 109, where also occurs a discussion of relaxation, pp. 101–107. The case of the impatient accountant appears in Wolpe, "Reciprocal Inhibition as the Main Basis of Psychotherapeutic Effects." pp. 93–94. Aubrey J. Yates, *Behavior Therapy,* p. 67, distinguishes between SD-I and SD-R techniques.

The case involving assertive therapy treatment is detailed in A. A. Lazarus, "New Methods in Psychotherapy," pp. 146–151. Types of problems treated by aversive therapy are described by Yates, *op. cit.,* pp. 234–239, and Eysenck's words of caution about the method appear in an introductory note in *Behaviour*

Therapy and the Neuroses, p. 277. Yates, *op. cit.*, provides summary examples of cases, pp. 235, 238, 319. The full case history is detailed in M. J. Raymond, "Case of Fetishism Treated by Aversion Therapy," pp. 303–311.

My chief source for the discussion of negative practice is G. F. J. Lehner, "Negative Practice as a Psychotherapeutic Technique," pp. 194–201. The case history entailing its use is found in H. W. Case, "Therapeutic Methods in Stuttering and Speech Blocking, pp. 212–213.

The Yates quotation on implosive therapy is in *op. cit.*, p. 70. The two brief case histories and the quoted comment occur in Wolpe, *The Practice of Behavior Therapy*, pp. 185–187. All of the examples of operant therapy are abstracted from James A. Sherman and Donald M. Baer, "Appraisal of Operant Therapy Techniques with Children and Adults," pp. 192–219.

Chapter Seven
The citations from B. F. Skinner, *Walden Two*, appear on pp. 260, 262, and 255–256, respectively. Perry London, *Behavior Control*, discusses individual awareness, pp. 269–271, 276–278; and the behavioral restraints on women and the consequences of the pill, pp. 215–217.

Bibliography

Bandura, Albert, "Psychotherapy as a Learning Process," *The Study of Abnormal Behavior,* ed. by Melvin Zax and George Stricker. New York: Macmillan Co., 1969. Pp. 329–346.

Case, H. W., "Therapeutic Methods in Stuttering and Speech Blocking," *Behaviour Therapy and the Neuroses,* ed. by H. J. Eysenck. Oxford: Pergamon Press, 1960. Pp. 207–220.

Dollard, John, and Neal E. Miller, *Personality and Psychotherapy.* New York: McGraw-Hill Book Co., 1950.

Eysenck, H. J., "Learning Theory and Behaviour Therapy," *Behaviour Therapy and the Neuroses,* ed. by H. J. Eysenck. Oxford: Pergamon Press, 1960. Pp. 4–21.

————, "Modern Learning Theory," *Behaviour Therapy and the Neuroses,* ed. by H. J. Eysenck. Oxford: Pergamon Press, 1960. Pp. 79–83.

Ferkiss, Victor C., *Technological Man: The Myth and the Reality.* New York: New American Library, 1970.

Ford, Donald H., and Hugh B. Urban, *Systems of Psychotherapy: A Comparative Study.* New York: John Wiley & Sons, 1963.

Franks, Cyril M., "Behavior Therapy and Its Pavlovian Origins," *Behavior Therapy: Appraisal and Status,* ed. by Cyril M. Franks. New York: McGraw-Hill Book Co., 1969. Pp. 1–26.

Franks, Cyril M., "Individual Differences in Conditioning and Associated Techniques," *The Conditioning Therapies,* ed. by Joseph Wolpe *et al.* New York: Holt, Rinehart & Winston, 1966. Pp. 149–165.

Hilgard, Ernest R., and Gordon H. Bower, *Theories of Learning* (3rd ed.). New York: Appleton-Century-Crofts, 1966.

Hill, Winfred F., *Learning: A Survey of Psychological Interpretations.* Scranton, Penna.: Chandler Publishing Co., 1963.

121

Kendrick, D. C., "The Theory of Conditioned Inhibition as an Explanation of Negative Practice Effects: An Experimental Analysis," *Behaviour Therapy and the Neuroses*, ed. by H. J. Eysenck. Oxford: Pergamon Press, 1960. Pp. 221–235.

Kimble, Gregory A., ed., *Foundations of Conditioning and Learning*. New York: Appleton-Century-Crofts, 1967.

Lazarus, A. A., "The Elimination of Children's Phobias by Deconditioning," *Behaviour Therapy and the Neuroses*, ed. by H. J. Eysenck. Oxford: Pergamon Press, 1960. Pp. 114–122.

——————, "New Methods in Psychotherapy: A Case Study," *Behaviour Therapy and the Neuroses*, ed. by H. J. Eysenck. Oxford: Pergamon Press, 1960. Pp. 144–152.

Lehner, G. F. J., "Negative Practice as a Psychotherapeutic Technique," *Behaviour Therapy and the Neuroses*, ed. by H. J. Eysenck. Oxford: Pergamon Press, 1960. Pp. 194–206.

London, Perry, *Behavior Control*. New York: Harper Perennial Library, 1971.

Meyer, V., and Edward S. Chesser, *Behaviour Therapy in Clinical Psychiatry*. Hammondsworth, Middlesex, England: Penguin Books, 1970.

Phillips, E. Larkin, and Daniel N. Wiener, *Short-Term Psychotherapy and Structured Behavior Change*. New York: McGraw-Hill Book Co., 1966.

Raymond, M. J., "Case of Fetishism Treated by Aversion Therapy," *Behaviour Therapy and the Neuroses*, ed. by H. J. Eysenck. Oxford: Pergamon Press, 1960. Pp. 303–311.

Razran, Gregory, *Mind in Evolution*. Boston: Houghton Mifflin, 1971.

Salter, Andrew, "The Theory and Practice of Conditioned Reflex Therapy," *The Conditioning Therapies*, ed. by Joseph Wolpe *et al*. New York: Holt, Rinehart & Winston, 1966. Pp. 21–37.

Sherman, James A., and Donald M. Baer, "Appraisal of Operant Therapy Techniques with Children and Adults," *Behavior Therapy: Appraisal and Status*, ed. by Cyril M. Franks. New York: McGraw-Hill Book Co., 1969. Pp. 192–219.

Skinner, B. F., *The Behavior of Organisms*. New York: Appleton-Century-Crofts, 1938.

——————, *Walden Two*. New York: Macmillan Co., 1962.

——————, *Beyond Freedom and Dignity*. New York: Alfred A. Knopf, 1971.

Suinn, Richard M., *Fundamentals of Behavior Pathology*. New York: John Wiley & Sons, 1970.

Walton, D., "The Application of Learning Theory to the Treatment of a Case of Neuro-Dermatitis," *Behaviour Therapy and the Neuroses,* ed. by H. J. Eysenck. Oxford: Pergamon Press, 1960. Pp. 272–274.

Watson, John B., and Rosalie Rayner, "Conditioned Emotional Reactions," *Journal of Experimental Psychology,* III, No. 1 (February, 1920), 1–14.

Watson, Robert I., *The Great Psychologists from Aristotle to Freud* (2nd ed.). Philadelphia: J. B. Lippincott Co., 1968.

Wolpe, Joseph, "The Comparative Clinical Status of Conditioning Therapies and Psychoanalysis," *The Conditioning Therapies,* ed. by Joseph Wolpe *et al.* New York: Holt, Rinehart & Winston, 1966. Pp. 5–20.

——————, *The Practice of Behavior Therapy.* New York: Pergamon Press, 1969.

——————, "Reciprocal Inhibition as the Main Basis of Psychotherapeutic Effects," *Behaviour Therapy and the Neuroses,* ed. by H. J. Eysenck. Oxford: Pergamon Press, 1960. Pp. 88–113.

Yates, Aubrey J., *Behavior Therapy.* New York: John Wiley & Sons, 1970.

INDEX

abnormal behavior, *see* behavior, abnormal

abnormal behavior, distinguished from normal, 63

abnormal psychology, 25

abnormalities, monosymptomatic, 66

abnormalities, polysymptomatic, 65

aggressiveness, 65

Albert B., *see* Little Albert experiment

alcoholism, 19; treatment of, 92

Americans, 58

analysis, social, 68

animal behavior, 59

Animal Intelligence, 37

animal phobia, 14

anorexia, treatment of, 101

anxiety, as a mediating drive, 64

assertive training, 89

autonomic reactivity, 65

aversion, conditioned, 71

aversive therapy, 91-2, 94-5

awareness, 110

bed wetting, *see* enuresis

behavior, abnormal, 22

behavior, criminal, 65

behavior modification, 14, 53

behavior, operant, 48-50

behavior, respondent, 48-9

behavior therapists, 64-5, 67, 71

behavior therapy, 62, 68, 70

behavior, voluntary, 54

behavioral psychologists, 70

behavioral psychology, 11-15, 19, 31, 47, 54-5, 59

behavioral science, 49, 63

Bernard, Claude, 20

bisexual cathexes, 58

Bower, *see* Hilgard and Bower

Brave New World, 106

California, University of, 56

case histories, 81-9, 92-8

cathexis, 58

centrality of drive, *see* drive, centrality of

Chicago, University of, 26

cigarette and liquor advertising, 53

classical conditioning, 22, 31, 38, 48

cognition, 56, 59

cognition modes, 58-9

cognition, theory of, 56

cognitive map, 58

cognitive phenomena, 59

Columbia University, 37

compulsions, 65

conditionability, differences in, 64

conditionability, level of, 66

conditioned aversion, *see* aversion, conditioned

conditioned inhibition, 45

conditioned reinforcers, 58

conditioned response, nature of, 24

conditioning, instrumental, 38

conditioning, phenomenon of, 22

conditioning, social, 68

contiguist school, 57

contiguity and recurrence, principles of, 33, 38

contiguity theorists, 38, 53, 55

contiguous conditioning, 32, 34

continuous reinforcement, 51

counter conditioning, *see* reciprocal inhibition

criminal behavior, *see* behavior, criminal

124